CELPIP WRITING PRACTICE
100 Questions & Answers

CELPIP WRITING TASK 1: WRITING AN EMAIL

1. You have recently moved to a new city and need to find a doctor.

In about 200 words, write an email to a friend asking for a recommendation for a doctor. Your message must include the following points:

1- An introduction to your situation and why you need a doctor.
2- A request for a recommendation for a good doctor in the area.
3- Any specific requirements or preferences for the doctor, such as specialization or location.
4- An expression of gratitude for their help.

Response:

Dear Joe,

I recently moved to Vancouver and I'm looking for a family doctor. Unfortunately, I'm not familiar with the healthcare system in this area and was hoping you could provide me with a recommendation.

I'm looking for a doctor who is knowledgeable and compassionate, and who takes the time to listen to their patients. I would prefer a doctor who specializes in family medicine and is located near my new residence in the downtown area.

If you have any personal experiences or recommendations for a doctor who meets these criteria, I would greatly appreciate your help. Your advice would help me in making an informed decision and ensure that I receive the best possible care.

Thank you in advance for your help. I look forward to hearing back from you soon.

Best regards,
David

2. You are a manager at a company and need to ask your colleague for a report.

In about 200 words, write an email to your colleague requesting a report on a recent project. Your message must include the following points:

1- A polite introduction and a mention of the project name.
2- A clear explanation of why you need the report and what you need to know.
3- A request for the report, including any deadlines or specific requirements.

Response:

Dear Sam,

I hope this email finds you well. I wanted to reach out to you regarding the [project name] that we worked on together last month. As you know, we completed the project within the deadline, and it was a great success.

However, I would like to request a report on the project's results, specifically regarding the project's financial performance and impact on customer satisfaction. This report would help us gain a better understanding of the project's outcomes and identify any areas of improvement for future projects.

I would appreciate it if you could provide me with this report by next Friday, the 22nd of April. Please let me know if you have any questions or if there are any other details I need to be aware of when creating this report.

Thank you in advance for your help with this matter. I look forward to reviewing the report and discussing it with you.

Best regards,
Joe

3. You are a student who needs to borrow a textbook from a classmate.

In about 200 words, write an email to your classmate asking to borrow their textbook. Your message must include the following points:

1- A polite greeting and introduction to the email.
2- An explanation of why you need to borrow their textbook and for how long.
3- A request to borrow the textbook and any specific details, such as which edition or author and an expression of gratitude and a promise to take good care of the textbook.

Response:

Dear Sarah,

I hope you're doing well. I'm writing to you because I am in need of a textbook for our [Course Name] class. I understand that you have a copy of the textbook, and I would appreciate it if I could borrow it from you.

I will need the textbook for the next two weeks to catch up on some reading and complete an upcoming assignment. If possible, I would like to borrow the third edition of the textbook written by [Author's Name]. I have checked with the school library, but unfortunately, they do not have a copy available for me to borrow.

I understand that lending out textbooks can be a personal matter, but I assure you that I will take good care of it and return it in the same condition in which I received it. If you would be willing to lend it to me, I can come to collect it at your convenience or arrange for you to drop it off at my dormitory.

Thank you for your consideration, and I look forward to hearing back from you soon.

Best regards,
Sam

4. You are a tenant who needs to inform your landlord about a problem in your apartment.

In about 200 words, write an email to your landlord reporting a leak in your bathroom. Your message must include the following points:

1- A polite greeting and an introduction to the email.
2- A clear description of the problem, including the location and severity of the leak.
3- A request for maintenance and an estimated timeframe for when the repair can be made.
4- A closing expression of gratitude and a promise to cooperate with the repair process.

Response:

Dear Matt,

I hope you are doing well. I am writing to inform you that I have noticed a leak in my bathroom, specifically from the showerhead. The leak appears to be coming from the piping behind the wall, and it has caused some water damage to the surrounding area.

I am writing to request your assistance in fixing the leak as soon as possible. I believe that this is a serious issue that requires attention, as the water damage has already caused some discoloration on the bathroom tiles. I would appreciate it if you could send a maintenance team to inspect the damage and make any necessary repairs.

I understand that you may have other maintenance requests to attend to, but if possible, I would like to have the repair done within the next week. I am available to schedule a time for the maintenance team to come by the apartment to make the repair, and I can provide you with my availability.

Thank you for your attention to this matter, and I appreciate your help in resolving this issue. I promise to cooperate with the repair process to ensure that everything goes smoothly.

Best regards,
Sarah

5. You are a recent university graduate seeking a job in your field.

In about 200 words, write an email to a potential employer expressing your interest in a job opening. Your message must include the following points:

1- A polite greeting and an introduction to the email.
2- An explanation of your qualifications, including your degree and any relevant experience.
3- An expression of interest in the job opening and an explanation of why you are a good fit for the position.
4- A closing expression of gratitude and an invitation for further communication.

Response:

Dear Sarah,

I hope this email finds you well. I am writing to express my interest in the recent job opening at your company for the position of [Job Title]. As a recent university graduate with a degree in [Field of Study], I believe that I would be a great fit for your team.

In addition to my academic background, I have had the opportunity to gain practical experience in the field through a previous internship at [Company Name], where I was able to develop my skills in [Specific Skill]. I have also worked on several projects that required me to collaborate with a team and apply my problem-solving skills.

I am particularly drawn to your company because of its reputation for innovation and its commitment to sustainability. I am eager to contribute my skills and knowledge to help advance these goals.

Thank you for considering my application. I have attached my resume and cover letter for your review. I would be happy to answer any questions or provide additional information about my qualifications. I look forward to hearing from you soon.

Best regards,
Matt

6. You recently attended a business conference and want to share your thoughts and ideas with your colleagues.

In about 200 words, write an email to your colleagues summarizing the conference and highlighting the key takeaways. Your message must include the following points:

1- A polite greeting and an introduction to the email.
2- A brief overview of the conference, including the topics covered and the speakers.
3- A summary of the key takeaways and insights gained from the conference.
4- An invitation to discuss the ideas further and an expression of excitement for future collaboration.

Response:

Dear Colleagues,

I hope this email finds you all doing well. I recently attended the business conference, which was held last week, and I wanted to share my thoughts and ideas with you all.

The conference was a great opportunity to hear from industry experts and learn about the latest trends and developments in our field. The topics covered included marketing strategies, innovation, and leadership, and the speakers were all highly engaging and informative.

One of the key takeaways from the conference was the importance of innovation in driving business growth. The speakers emphasized the need for companies to be agile and adaptable in order to stay competitive in today's market. Another important insight was the role of social media in building brand awareness and engaging with customers.

I am excited to discuss these ideas further with all of you and explore how we can apply them to our work. I believe that by working together, we can leverage these insights to drive innovation and growth for our company.

Thank you for taking the time to read my email. I look forward to hearing your thoughts and ideas on these topics.

Best regards,
Matt

7. You have recently moved to a new neighborhood and would like to introduce yourself to your new neighbors.

In about 200 words, write an email to your new neighbors introducing yourself and expressing your excitement to be part of the community. Your message must include the following points:

1- A polite greeting and an introduction to the email.
2- A brief introduction about yourself, your family, and your interests.
3- An expression of excitement to be part of the community and an invitation to connect.
4- A closing remark and a polite farewell.

Response:

Dear New Neighbors,

I hope this email finds you all doing well. My family and I recently moved into the neighborhood, and I wanted to take this opportunity to introduce myself and express my excitement to be part of the community.

My name is Sarah and I live with my husband and two children, Alex and Emily. We have always loved the charm and friendliness of this neighborhood, and we are thrilled to finally call it our home.

In my free time, I enjoy gardening and reading, and my husband is an avid cyclist. Alex is a talented artist, and Emily loves playing soccer. We are all looking forward to exploring the neighborhood and meeting new people.

We feel fortunate to be part of such a warm and welcoming community, and we are excited to get to know our new neighbors. Please don't hesitate to reach out if you have any questions or if you'd like to connect. We would love to get to know you all.

Thank you for taking the time to read my email. We look forward to meeting you soon!

Best regards,
Sarah

8. You recently visited a hotel and you were dissatisfied with your stay. Write an email to the hotel manager outlining your concerns.

In about 200 words, write an email to the hotel manager expressing your dissatisfaction and outlining the specific issues you experienced. Your message must include the following points:

1- A polite greeting and introduction to the email.
2- A clear description of the problems you experienced during your stay.
3- A request for a resolution or compensation.
4- A closing remark and a polite farewell.

Response:

Dear Hotel Manager,

I hope this email finds you well. I recently stayed at your hotel, and unfortunately, I had a very disappointing experience.

Firstly, the room was not clean upon my arrival. The bathroom had hair in the sink and bathtub, and there was dust on the furniture. Additionally, the air conditioning unit was not functioning correctly, making it difficult to sleep comfortably.

Furthermore, the noise level in the hotel was extremely high, and it was difficult to relax or get any work done. The doors in the hallway were slamming constantly, and there were people talking loudly at all hours of the night.

As a paying customer, I was very disappointed with the overall quality of my stay. I would appreciate a resolution or compensation for the issues I experienced during my time at the hotel.

Thank you for taking the time to read my email, and I look forward to hearing from you soon.

Best regards,
Sam

9. You are a member of a team organizing an event for your company. Write an email to your team members with details of the event.

In about 200 words, write an email to your team members with all the necessary details of the event. Your message must include the following points:

1- A polite greeting and introduction to the email.
2- The date, time, and location of the event.
3- A brief description of the event, including its purpose and expected outcomes.
4- Any instructions or requests for the team members regarding their roles in the event.
5- A closing remark and a polite farewell.

Response:

Dear Team Members,

I hope this email finds you all doing well. I am excited to share the details of the upcoming event that we are organizing for our company.

The event will take place on Saturday, May 7th, at the Grand Hotel from 6 PM to 10 PM. The Grand Hotel is located in the heart of downtown, and we have reserved the banquet hall for our event.

The purpose of this event is to celebrate our company's recent achievements and to provide an opportunity for our employees to connect and network with each other. We expect a turnout of around 100 guests, including employees, their families, and some VIPs.

As a member of the organizing team, I would like to request that you arrive at the venue by 5 PM for setup and final preparations. We will have a detailed timeline of the evening's events, and I would like to request that you assist with tasks such as greeting guests, managing registration, and ensuring that everyone is having a great time.

Thank you for your hard work and dedication to making this event a success. I am looking forward to working with you all and to having a great time at the event.

Best regards,
Sam

10. You have recently stayed at a hotel and were not satisfied with the service provided. Write an email to the hotel manager to complain about the issues.

In about 200 words, write an email to the hotel manager to complain about the issues that you faced during your stay. Your message must include the following points:

1- A polite greeting and introduction to the email.
2- The details of the issues that you faced during your stay, including the date and room number.
3- How the issues affected your stay and any inconvenience caused.
4- Any suggestions or requests to resolve the issues.
5- A closing remark and a polite farewell.

Response:

Dear Mr.Johnson,

I hope this email finds you well. I am writing to you regarding my recent stay at your hotel. Unfortunately, I was disappointed with the service provided during my stay.

I stayed in room 204 from April 3rd to April 6th. The first issue that I faced was that the room was not properly cleaned when I arrived. The bathroom had hair on the floor, and there were stains on the bed sheets. Additionally, the air conditioning in the room was not working properly, and it made a loud noise throughout the night.

The issues with the room affected my stay, and I was not able to sleep comfortably during my stay. The inconvenience caused by the lack of cleanliness and the noise from the air conditioning made it difficult to enjoy my time at the hotel.

I would appreciate it if you could take appropriate steps to ensure that such issues are not faced by other guests in the future. I suggest that you conduct regular checks of the rooms and improve the maintenance of the air conditioning units.

Thank you for your attention to this matter. I hope that my feedback will help you improve the service provided by your hotel.

Sincerely,
Sarah

11. You recently attended a conference and would like to thank the organizers for their efforts.

In about 200 words, write an email to the organizers of the conference to thank them for their hard work and for organizing such a successful event. Your message must include the following points:

1- A polite greeting and introduction to the email.
2- A statement about the conference and the reason for attending.
3- A compliment to the organizers and their efforts in organizing the conference.
4- A brief overview of the highlights of the conference.
5- A closing remark and a polite farewell.

Response:

Dear Conference Organizers,

I hope this email finds you well. I am writing to express my sincere gratitude for organizing such an informative and well-planned conference. It was an excellent opportunity to learn from experts in the field, and I am grateful for the opportunity to attend.

The conference was held from April 10th to April 12th, and I attended as a representative of my company. The topics covered were highly relevant to my work, and I was able to gain a deeper understanding of current trends and best practices.

I want to compliment the organizers for their efforts in planning and executing the conference. The sessions were well-organized, and the speakers were highly knowledgeable and engaging. The venue and facilities were also top-notch, making the conference a highly enjoyable experience.

One of the highlights of the conference was the panel discussion on the future of the industry, which provided valuable insights and sparked interesting discussions. The networking opportunities were also valuable, allowing me to meet and connect with other professionals in the field.

Once again, thank you for your hard work and dedication in organizing this conference. It was an enriching experience, and I look forward to attending future events organized by your team.

Sincerely,
Sam

12. You are organizing a charity event for a local cause.

In about 200 words, write an email to your friends and colleagues to invite them to participate in the event. Your message must include the following points:

1- An introduction to the event and the cause it supports.
2- A brief overview of the activities planned for the event.
3- The date, time, and location of the event.
4- A request for their participation and support.
5- Contact information for further inquiries.

Response:

Dear Friends and Colleagues,

I am writing to invite you to a charity event that I am organizing to support a local cause. The event will be a fun-filled day of activities for all ages, and all proceeds will go towards supporting the cause.

The cause we are supporting is a local shelter for homeless youth. This shelter provides a safe haven and resources for young people who are experiencing homelessness, and they rely on donations to keep their programs running.

The event will include a bake sale, a silent auction, and a variety of games and activities for children and adults alike. We will also have live music and food trucks to make it a fun and enjoyable day for everyone.

The event will take place on May 15th from 10 am to 4 pm at the local park on Main Street. I would be honoured if you could join us in supporting this worthy cause. Your participation and support are crucial in making this event a success.

If you have any questions or would like to contribute in any way, please feel free to contact me at [insert contact information]. I look forward to seeing you at the event!

Best regards,
[Your Name]

13. You are an employee in a company and you want to request a day off for personal reasons.

In about 200 words, write an email to your supervisor requesting the day off. Your message must include the following points:

1- A clear and polite request for the day off.
2- The reason for your request.
3- The date you are requesting off.
4- Any necessary information about your work schedule and responsibilities, including any arrangements you have made to ensure your tasks are covered in your absence.
5- Your contact information for follow-up.

Response:

Dear [Supervisor's Name],

I hope this email finds you well. I am writing to request a day off for personal reasons. I would like to take off Friday, May 21st.

I understand that this is short notice and that my absence may cause some inconvenience to the team. However, I have made arrangements to ensure that my tasks will be covered during my absence. I have already briefed my colleague [Name of the colleague] on my work schedule and responsibilities, and he/she has agreed to take over my tasks while I am away.

The reason for my request is that I have a family event out of town that I need to attend. My attendance is important for the family, and I would be grateful if you could grant me the day off. I assure you that I will complete all my tasks and duties before leaving and that I will make up for any missed work upon my return.

Please let me know if there is anything else I can do to ensure that my absence does not affect the team's productivity. I appreciate your understanding and look forward to hearing from you.

If you need to contact me for any reason, please feel free to reach out to me on my cell phone at [Your phone number] or by email at [Your email address].

Thank you for your time and consideration.

Sincerely,
[Your Name]

14. You recently attended a training session and you want to thank the trainer.

In about 200 words, write an email to the trainer thanking them for the training session. Your message must include the following points:

1- An opening sentence thanking the trainer.
2- The specific things you learned from the training session and how they will be useful to you.
3- How did the trainer's presentation style help you understand the material better?
4- A closing sentence expressing your gratitude again.

Response:

Dear [Trainer's Name],

I hope this email finds you well. I recently attended your training session on [Training Session Name], and I wanted to take a moment to express my gratitude for the knowledge and insights you shared.

Thank you for the excellent training session. Your knowledge and expertise in the subject matter were impressive, and I was impressed by the depth of your understanding of the material. I especially appreciated the way you presented the material, which made it easy to understand and retain.

The training session provided me with specific and practical tools that I can apply to my job. Your explanations and examples were clear, concise, and relevant, and I left the session feeling more confident in my ability to apply the concepts learned.

Your presentation style was engaging and dynamic, and it kept me focused and interested throughout the session. Your use of real-life examples and case studies helped me understand the material better, and I appreciated the interactive approach you took to the session.

Thank you once again for sharing your knowledge and expertise with us. The session was extremely valuable, and I look forward to applying what I learned in my work.

Sincerely,
[Your Name]

15. You are a student and you want to request a meeting with your professor to discuss an assignment.

In about 200 words, write an email to your professor requesting a meeting to discuss your assignment. Your message must include the following points:

1- A polite greeting and introduction.
2- A brief description of the assignment you want to discuss.
3- The reason why you want to meet and what you hope to achieve.
4- A request for a meeting time that is convenient for both of you.

Response:

Dear Professor [Last Name],

I hope this email finds you well. I am writing to request a meeting with you to discuss my recent assignment on [Assignment Name].

I would appreciate the opportunity to meet with you to review my assignment and get feedback on how I can improve my work. I want to ensure that I am meeting the expectations of the course and fulfilling the requirements of the assignment to the best of my ability.

I would like to discuss the specific areas where I struggled and receive guidance on how to improve. I am also open to any suggestions you may have on how to approach future assignments to ensure that I am meeting the learning objectives of the course.

Please let me know if you are available for a meeting sometime next week. I am available on [Days and times you are available], but I am also flexible and can work around your schedule.

Thank you for your time and consideration, and I look forward to hearing from you soon.

Sincerely,
[Your Name]

16. You are a manager at a hotel and a guest has complained about their recent stay.

In about 200 words, write an email to the guest addressing their concerns and offering a solution. Your message must include the following points:

1- An apology for their negative experience.
2- An acknowledgment of the specific issue(s) they raised.
3- A proposed solution to address their concerns.
4- A closing statement that thanks them for bringing the issue to your attention and encourages them to visit again.

Response:

Dear Mr. Johnson,

I am writing to apologize for the negative experience you had during your recent stay at our hotel. We take all guest feedback seriously, and I am sorry to hear that we did not meet your expectations.

I understand that you experienced issues with the cleanliness of your room and noise from other guests. Please know that this is not typical of the level of service and comfort we aim to provide to our guests.

To address your concerns, I have spoken with our housekeeping staff to ensure that our cleaning standards are being upheld and that all rooms are thoroughly inspected before guest check-in. Additionally, I have instructed our front desk staff to take extra precautions when assigning rooms to ensure that guests are not placed near any noise disturbances.

As a token of our appreciation for your feedback, I would like to offer you a complimentary night's stay on your next visit. We value your business and hope that you will consider staying with us again.

Thank you again for bringing this issue to our attention, and please do not hesitate to contact me directly if you have any further concerns or feedback.

Sincerely,

[Your Name]
Hotel Manager

17. You have received a job offer from a company, but you have some questions before accepting the offer.

In about 200 words, write an email to the HR representative who sent you the offer. Your message must include the following points:

1- Thanking them for the job offer.
2- Your questions about the job or the company.
3- A request for clarification or additional information.
4- A closing statement expressing your enthusiasm about the opportunity.

Response:

Dear Ms. Johnson,

I would like to thank you for extending a job offer to me to join your team at XYZ Company. I am thrilled at the prospect of working with your company, and I appreciate the confidence you have placed in me.

Before I can make a final decision, I have a few questions regarding the position and the company that I hope you can provide some clarity on. Firstly, could you provide me with more information regarding the job responsibilities and requirements? I would like to have a better understanding of the day-to-day tasks and expectations of the position.

Secondly, I am curious to know more about the company's culture and values. As an employee, I am interested in knowing how the company approaches work-life balance and employee development.

Lastly, I was wondering if there are any additional benefits or perks that are not mentioned in the offer letter. This information would be helpful in evaluating the overall compensation package.

Thank you for considering my questions. I am excited about the opportunity to join your team, and I appreciate your time and effort in answering my queries. I look forward to hearing back from you soon.

Sincerely,

[Your Name]

18. You recently stayed at a hotel and had a problem during your stay.

In about 200 words, write an email to the hotel manager to describe the problem and request a solution. Your message must include the following points:

1- A brief explanation of your stay at the hotel and the problem you experienced.
2- The impact of the problem on your experience.
3- A request for a solution to the problem.
4- A closing statement expressing your appreciation for their help.

Response:

Dear Mr. Brown,

I recently had the pleasure of staying at the Sunflower Hotel during my visit to your city. Overall, my stay was quite pleasant, but I did experience a problem that I hope you can help me resolve.

On the second night of my stay, I discovered that the air conditioning in my room was not working properly. Despite adjusting the thermostat and waiting for some time, the temperature did not seem to improve. I informed the front desk, but unfortunately, the issue was not resolved during my stay.

The lack of air conditioning had a significant impact on my comfort during the night, and I found it difficult to sleep properly. As a result, my overall experience at the hotel was not as enjoyable as it could have been.

I would like to request a solution to this problem, such as a partial refund or a discount on a future stay at your hotel. I hope we can come to an agreement that will satisfy both of us.

Thank you for your time and attention to this matter. I

appreciate your help in resolving this issue and look forward to hearing from you soon.

Sincerely,

[Your Name]

19. You are a manager of a retail store. Your store recently received a negative review online.

In about 200 words, write an email to the customer who left the negative review, addressing their concerns and offering a solution. Your message must include the following points:

1- A sincere apology for their negative experience.
2- An acknowledgement of the specific concerns they raised in their review.
3- A proposed solution to address their concerns.
4- A closing statement expressing your appreciation for their feedback and offering your assistance if needed.

Response:

Dear Ms. Johnson,

I would like to personally apologize for the negative experience you had at our store, as well as the delay in responding to your online review. Your feedback is extremely important to us, and we take all reviews seriously.

I understand your frustration with the long wait time at the checkout counter and the lack of available staff to assist you. We have recently experienced a higher volume of customers than usual, which has unfortunately resulted in longer wait times and a shortage of staff during peak hours.

To address your concerns, we are taking immediate action to hire more staff and increase our training programs to ensure that all employees are equipped to provide excellent customer service. Additionally, we will be implementing new technology to improve the checkout process and reduce wait times.

As a token of our appreciation for your feedback and to regain your trust in our store, I would like to offer you a 20% discount on your next purchase with us. Please feel free to contact me directly if you have any further concerns or suggestions for improvement.

Thank you again for taking the time to provide us with your feedback. We value your business and hope to have the opportunity to provide you with a better experience in the future.

Sincerely,

[Your Name]
Store Manager, XYZ Retail Store

20. You are a university student who missed a final exam due to illness.

In about 200 words, write an email to your professor, explaining the situation and requesting a makeup exam. Your message must include the following points:

1- An explanation for missing the exam.
2- A request to schedule a makeup exam.
3- An acknowledgement of any inconvenience caused.
4- A closing statement expressing your appreciation for their understanding.

Response:

Dear Professor Johnson,

I am writing to inform you that I was unable to attend the final exam for your course, due to an unexpected illness. I understand the importance of the final exam and the impact that missing it may have on my grade. I apologize for any inconvenience this may cause.

I was feeling unwell the night before the exam and attempted to study, but was unable to focus due to the severity of my symptoms. I had hoped to recover in time to attend the exam, but unfortunately, my condition worsened, and I was advised by my doctor to rest at home.

I would like to request the opportunity to make up the final exam at the earliest convenience. I understand that scheduling a makeup exam may be challenging, but I am willing to work with you to find a suitable time and location. I am willing to complete the exam under any conditions that you may deem necessary, such as supervision or time constraints.

Again, I apologize for any inconvenience caused and appreciate your understanding in this matter. Thank you for your time and consideration.

Sincerely,

[Your Name]
University Student, XYZ University

21. You recently purchased a defective product from an online retailer.

In about 200 words, write an email to the retailer's customer service department, explaining the problem and requesting a refund or replacement. Your message must include:

1- A description of the product and the issue.
2- The date of purchase and the order number.
3- A request for a refund or replacement.
4- An acknowledgement of any inconvenience caused.

Response:

Dear Customer Service,

I am writing to report a problem with a product that I purchased from your online store. On the 15th of March, I ordered a set of wireless headphones from your website, with order number #12345. Unfortunately, I have discovered that the product is defective.

Upon receiving the headphones, I immediately noticed that the sound quality was poor, and there was a constant hissing noise that was present during playback. Despite multiple attempts to troubleshoot the issue, I was unable to resolve the problem. I am extremely disappointed as I was excited to try out this product.

As the product is faulty, I would like to request a refund or a replacement. I understand that returning the product may cause some inconvenience, but I hope that you can understand my frustration and the need for a resolution.

Please let me know how I can proceed with this request. I would appreciate a prompt response as I would like to resolve this issue as soon as possible. Thank you for your time and attention to this matter.

Sincerely,

[Your Name]
Customer

22. You recently attended a conference in another city.

In about 200 words, write an email to your supervisor, summarizing what you learned at the conference and how it could be useful for your company. Your message must include the following points:

1- The name and location of the conference.
2- The date of the conference.
3- The key topics or themes discussed.
4- How the information gained could be applied to your company.

Response:

Dear [Supervisor's Name],

I am writing to give you a summary of the recent conference that I attended in Vancouver. The conference was the International Business Summit, which took place from May 15th to May 17th at the Vancouver Convention Centre.

The conference covered a range of topics related to global business trends and emerging markets. Some of the key themes included the impact of technology on international trade, the role of sustainability in business, and strategies for entering new markets.

I found the conference to be extremely informative and valuable. The sessions provided insights and ideas that could be applied to our company. For instance, the discussion on the role of sustainability in business made me think about how we can integrate more sustainable practices in our operations, and the session on strategies for entering new markets gave me some ideas for expanding our business to new regions.

Overall, I believe that attending this conference has broadened my understanding of the global business landscape and equipped me with new ideas that can benefit our company.

I would highly recommend attending this conference in the future.

Thank you for considering my report.

Sincerely,

[Your Name]

23. Complaint about a hotel stay.

In about 200 words, write an email to the manager of a hotel you recently stayed at, outlining your complaints about your stay. Your message must include the following points:

1- The dates of your stay.
2- The room number and type of room you stayed in.
3- Specific complaints about the room or services provided.
4- What you would like the manager to do to address the issues.

Response:

Dear Manager,

I am writing to express my disappointment with my recent stay at your hotel. I stayed at your establishment from May 20th to May 22nd in room 305, which was booked as a deluxe queen room.

Unfortunately, my experience was far from deluxe. The room was small and cramped, with barely enough space to move around. The bathroom was not cleaned properly, with hair left in the sink and bathtub. The air conditioning was not functioning properly, making the room hot and stuffy. In addition, the noise from the street outside was so loud that I could barely sleep.

Given the high cost of the room, I expected a much better experience. I would like to request that you take immediate action to address these issues. I suggest that you provide a refund for the cost of the room or a complimentary future stay to make up for the inconvenience.

I hope that you take my complaints seriously and take steps to ensure that other guests do not experience the same issues. Thank you for your attention to this matter.

Sincerely,

[Your Name]

24. Request for a reference letter

In about 200 words, write an email to a former employer asking for a reference letter for a job application. Your message must include the following points:

1- An introduction to yourself and your current job search.
2- A reminder of the work you did for the employer and when you worked for them.
3- A request for a reference letter and the job or program you are applying for.
4- Any additional information or instructions you would like the employer to include in the letter.

Response:

Dear [Employer's Name],

I hope this email finds you well. I am writing to request a reference letter for a job application that I am currently pursuing. I am seeking a position in [industry/field] and would greatly appreciate your support.

I worked for your company as a [position] from [start date] to [end date], and I am proud to say that I learned so much during my time there. I enjoyed working with the team and was able to contribute to various projects and initiatives.

I would be grateful if you could provide me with a reference letter highlighting my skills and accomplishments during my time at your company. The job I am applying for requires strong communication and project management skills, and I believe that my experience with your company has prepared me well for this role.

If possible, could you please include any specific examples or projects that showcase my skills and experience? I would also appreciate any guidance on what to expect during the hiring process, as I know that you have a wealth of experience in the industry.

Thank you for your time and consideration. I look forward to hearing back from you soon.

Best regards,

[Your Name]

25. Complaint Letter to Landlord

In about 200 words, write an email to your landlord complaining about a problem in your apartment. Your message must include the following points:

1- An introduction stating the problem you are experiencing.
2- A description of the impact the problem is having on your life.
3- A request for a solution or action to be taken.
4- A polite closing.

Response:

Dear [Landlord's Name],

I am writing to bring to your attention a problem that has been affecting me for some time now. The problem is with the heating system in my apartment. Despite my repeated attempts to fix the issue, the heating system still does not work properly, and it is having a significant impact on my daily life.

The lack of heating in my apartment has made it almost impossible for me to carry out my daily activities comfortably. I am constantly feeling cold, and it is difficult to get a good night's sleep in such conditions. Moreover, the low temperature has caused the pipes to freeze, and this has resulted in damage to my furniture and other belongings.

I would appreciate it if you could take immediate action to resolve this problem. I understand that the issue may require some time and resources to fix, but I cannot continue to live in these conditions. If possible, could you please let me know the timeline for when the problem will be fixed, so that I can plan accordingly?

Thank you for your attention to this matter. I look forward to hearing from you soon.

Sincerely,

[Your Name]

26. Requesting Time Off Work

In about 200 words, write an email to your manager requesting time off work. Your message must include the following points:

1- An introduction stating the reason for the request.
2- The specific dates you are requesting off.
3- A brief explanation of how you plan to make up for any missed work or ensure that your tasks are covered while you are away.
4- A polite closing.

Response:

Dear [Manager's Name],

I am writing to request some time off from work. My sister is getting married in another state, and I would like to attend the wedding. The wedding is on Saturday, May 28, and I would need to take Thursday and Friday off as well to travel there and prepare for the event.

I understand that this is a busy time for our department, but I have already spoken to my team members, and they have agreed to help cover my work while I am away. I have also made arrangements to ensure that all of my current projects are completed or handed over to other team members before I leave.

I am more than happy to work overtime or come in early during the week leading up to my time off to make up for any missed work. I also plan to be available by phone and email during my time off in case of any urgent matters that may require my attention.

Thank you for your consideration of my request. Please let me know if there is anything else I can do to ensure a smooth transition while I am away.

Sincerely,

[Your Name]

.

27. You are a manager of a retail store. Write an email to your staff regarding a new policy.

In about 200 words, write an email to your staff about a new policy that the company is implementing. Your message should include the following points:

1- Explain the new policy.
2- Provide the reasons for implementing the new policy.
3- Outline how the policy will affect the staff and the company.

Response:

Dear Team,

I am writing to inform you about an important change that is being made to our store policies. Effective immediately, we are implementing a new policy for handling returns and exchanges.

The new policy will require all customers to present a receipt or proof of purchase when returning or exchanging an item. This policy is being put in place to protect our company from potential losses due to fraudulent returns, as well as to ensure that our inventory is accurately tracked and managed.

We understand that this policy may cause some inconvenience for our customers and for our staff, as it may require additional time and effort to verify receipts and process returns. However, we believe that it is necessary to maintain the integrity of our business and to provide the best service possible to our customers.

To help our staff adjust to the new policy, we will be providing training and resources to ensure that everyone is familiar with the new procedures. Additionally, we will closely monitor how the policy affects our business and make adjustments as necessary to ensure that we continue to provide the best service possible.

Thank you for your understanding and cooperation during this transition.

Sincerely,

[Your Name]
Store Manager

28. You are an employee in a company. Your team is planning a weekend retreat.

In about 200 words, write an email to your team members to finalize the date and location of the retreat. Your message must include the following points:

1- Introduction and purpose of the email.
2- Possible dates for the retreat.
3- Possible locations for the retreat.
4- Activities and itinerary for the retreat.
5- Conclusion and request for feedback.

Response:

Dear Team,

I hope this email finds you well. As discussed in our last team meeting, we are planning a weekend retreat to foster team-building and relaxation. I am writing to finalize the date and location of the retreat, and to request your feedback on the itinerary.

For the dates, we have three possible weekends in mind: August 14-15, August 21-22, or August 28-29. Please let me know your availability for these dates so we can finalize the best weekend for all of us.

As for the location, we have narrowed down the options to two: Banff and Jasper National Parks. Both parks have beautiful scenic views and offer a range of outdoor activities. Please let me know which location you prefer, and if you have any other suggestions.

For activities and itineraries, we have a few ideas in mind such as hiking, camping, and rafting. We also plan to have some team-building exercises and a bonfire night. Please let me know if you have any other suggestions or preferences.

In conclusion, I would like to thank you for your participation in the planning process so far. I look forward to your feedback so we can finalize the date, location, and itinerary. Please respond to this email with your feedback and any questions you may have.

Best regards,
[Your Name]

29. Request for information about an English course.

In about 200 words, write an email to a language school to inquire about their English courses. Your message must include the following points:

1- Introduction and reason for writing
2- Information about the courses offered
3- Schedule and location of the courses
4- Cost of the courses and payment options

Response:

Dear Sir/Madam,

I am writing to inquire about the English courses offered at your language school. I am interested in improving my English language skills, as it is essential for my job and personal growth.

Could you please provide me with information about the courses offered? I would appreciate it if you could provide details on the course structure, levels, and duration. I am looking for a course that is both challenging and effective in improving my English proficiency.

I would also like to know the schedule and location of the courses. Are the classes held during the day or evening? Are they held on weekdays or weekends? I work full-time, so I need a course schedule that is flexible and can accommodate my work schedule. Additionally, I would like to know if the courses are offered online or in person.

Finally, I would appreciate it if you could provide me with information about the cost of the courses and payment options. Do you offer any discounts or scholarships? Can I pay for the course in installments, or do I need to pay the full amount upfront?

Thank you for taking the time to read my email. I look forward to hearing from you soon.

Sincerely,
John Doe

30. You are the manager of a retail store. There is a new shopping mall opening near your store.

In about 200 words, write to your staff and ask for suggestions on how your store can attract new customers when the shopping mall opens. Your message must include the following points:

1- A brief explanation of the situation.
2- A request for suggestions on how to attract new customers.
3- A reminder of the importance of customer service and why it is important.
4- A note on when you would like to receive suggestions.

Response:

Dear team,

As you are all aware, the new shopping mall is opening up just a few blocks away from our store. This is a major event that is expected to attract a lot of customers, and we need to be prepared to compete for their business.

I would like to take this opportunity to ask for your suggestions on how we can attract new customers to our store. We need to be creative and proactive in our approach, and I believe that your ideas will be invaluable in achieving this.

While we brainstorm on how to attract new customers, it's important to remember that customer service is our top priority. We pride ourselves on providing excellent service to our customers, and this will be crucial in retaining our existing customer base and attracting new ones.

I encourage all of you to take some time to think about how we can make our store stand out in this competitive environment. Please send your suggestions to me via email by the end of the week, so that we can discuss them at our next team meeting.

Thank you for your dedication and hard work.

Best regards,
[Your Name]

31. You are an employee at a travel agency. One of your customers is unhappy with their recent vacation.

In about 200 words, write an email to your customer in response to their complaint. Your message must include the following points:

1- Acknowledge their complaint.
2- Apologize for their experience.
3- Explain what may have gone wrong.
4- Offer a solution to their issue.
5- Invite them to return.

Response:

Dear Mr. Johnson,

I'm sorry to hear that your recent vacation was not satisfactory. As a valued customer, it's important that we meet your expectations, and in this case, it seems we fell short.

I apologize for any inconvenience or disappointment caused by the issues you experienced. After looking into your complaint, it appears that there was an issue with the hotel room you were assigned to. We acknowledge that it wasn't up to the standards we promised you.

Please know that we take this matter seriously, and have already taken steps to prevent similar situations from happening in the future. As a goodwill gesture, we would like to offer you a complimentary stay at a different location of your choice, with all expenses covered. We hope this will help make up for the unfortunate events on your last vacation.

We would love to have you back as a customer, and we hope that this offer will demonstrate our commitment to providing you with the best experience possible. Please let us know if you have any questions, or if there's anything else we can do for you.

Best regards,

Jane Smith
Customer Service Representative
Sunshine Travel Agency

32. You recently stayed in a hotel and were dissatisfied with the service.

In about 200 words, write an email to the manager of the hotel to express your dissatisfaction and suggest some improvements. Your message must include the following points:

1- An introduction to the problem and what happened.
2- The specific reasons for your dissatisfaction with the service.
3- Your suggestions for how the hotel could improve.
4- A request for a response from the manager.

Response:

Dear Manager,

I recently stayed at your hotel, the Plaza Inn, and unfortunately, my experience was not up to my expectations. I would like to express my dissatisfaction with the service I received during my stay.

The first issue I encountered was upon checking in. The front desk staff seemed disorganized and unprepared. I had to wait in line for over 20 minutes while they dealt with other guests. Once I finally got to the desk, the check-in process was slow and tedious.

Additionally, the cleanliness of the room left much to be desired. There were stains on the carpet, the sheets were not properly cleaned, and the bathroom was in need of a deep clean.

To improve the hotel, I suggest implementing a more efficient check-in process and ensuring that the housekeeping staff properly cleans the rooms. I also recommend that the hotel invest in new bedding and carpets to maintain a high level of comfort and cleanliness for guests.

I hope that you take these suggestions into consideration and take action to improve the overall quality of the hotel. Thank you for your time and attention to this matter.

Sincerely,
[Your Name]

33. Request for information about a volunteer opportunity

In about 200 words, write an email to a non-profit organization asking about volunteer opportunities. Your message must include the following points:

1- Introduction and a brief explanation of your interest in volunteering.
2- The type of volunteer work you are interested in and why.
3- The time and duration you are available to volunteer.
4- Any relevant experience or skills you have.

Response:

Dear Sir/Madam,

I am writing to inquire about volunteer opportunities available at your non-profit organization. I came across your organization's website while searching for ways to give back to my community, and I am excited to learn more about the work you do.

I am interested in working with children and helping to organize after-school programs. I believe that providing a safe and nurturing environment for children to learn and grow is crucial for their future success. I have previously volunteered with a local community center and helped to organize a summer camp for children, and I found it to be an incredibly rewarding experience.

I am available to volunteer on weekends and weekday evenings, and I would be willing to commit to at least six hours per week. I am flexible and would be happy to discuss any opportunities you may have available that fit my schedule.

In terms of my relevant experience, I have previously worked with children in a variety of settings, including as a tutor and mentor. I am also comfortable working with technology and would be happy to help with any administrative tasks that may be needed.

Thank you for considering my application. I look forward to hearing back from you soon.

Sincerely,
John Smith

34. You are the manager of a clothing store. One of your employees has been underperforming and making several mistakes.

You need to write an email to this employee to address the issue. In about 200 words, write an email that includes the following points:

1- Explain the specific mistakes that have been made.
2- Explain why these mistakes are problematic for the business.
3- Provide clear instructions on how the employee can improve their performance.
4- End the email with a positive statement that encourages the employee to do better.

Response:

Dear [Employee Name],

I am writing to address some concerns about your recent performance at the store. Specifically, there have been several mistakes that you have made in the past week, including failing to complete inventory checks and incorrectly labeling items. These mistakes have led to discrepancies in our records and have caused confusion among both our staff and customers.

As I'm sure you understand, these mistakes are problematic for our business. Inaccurate records can lead to a loss of inventory, and incorrectly labeled items can lead to customer dissatisfaction and potential loss of sales. I want to work with you to make sure these issues are resolved.

To help improve your performance, please review the store policies and procedures manual. Take your time to understand the correct procedures for inventory checks and labeling items. Please ask your colleagues or me if you have any questions or need further clarification.

I believe in your ability to perform well and contribute to

our team. Your past contributions have been valuable and appreciated, and I know that you have the potential to improve in these areas. Please let me know if there is anything else I can do to support you in achieving your goals.

Best regards,
[Your Name]

35. You are the manager of a restaurant. One of your regular customers has written to you to express their disappointment with their recent experience.

In about 200 words, write an email to this customer in response to their complaint. Your message must include the following points:

1- An apology for their negative experience.
2- An explanation of what went wrong.
3- An assurance that the issue has been resolved.
4- An invitation for them to return to the restaurant.

Response:

Dear Mr. Johnson,

I was sorry to hear that your recent visit to our restaurant did not meet your expectations. I would like to extend my apologies on behalf of our entire team for any inconvenience or frustration you experienced.

We pride ourselves on providing exceptional food and service to our customers, and it is clear that we failed to deliver on that promise during your last visit. After investigating the matter, it appears that we were understaffed that evening, which caused longer wait times and resulted in your food not being prepared to our usual standards.

Please know that we have since addressed this issue by hiring additional staff members and refining our scheduling practices. We are committed to ensuring that all of our customers receive the high-quality experience they deserve, and we will do everything we can to ensure that such issues do not occur again in the future.

We would like to invite you to return to our restaurant and give us the opportunity to make it up to you. We value your business and would love the chance to show you the level of service and quality that we are capable of providing.

Thank you for taking the time to bring your concerns to our attention, and we look forward to the opportunity to serve you again soon.

Sincerely,

[Your Name]
Manager, [Restaurant Name]

36. You are a college student and you need to inform your professor about missing class.

In about 200 words, write an email to your professor informing them about why you cannot attend class, the steps you have taken to stay on track, and a plan to catch up on the missed material.

Response:

Dear Professor Brown,

I am writing to inform you that I will not be able to attend your class on Wednesday, September 15th, as I have to attend a family emergency out of town. I apologize for any inconvenience this may cause and would like to request permission to make up the missed work.

To ensure that I stay on track with the course, I have already read the assigned chapters in the textbook and reviewed the lecture notes that are posted online. Furthermore, I have reached out to a few of my classmates to request their notes from the class that I will be missing.

I am aware that we will be covering new material during this class, and I am eager to catch up on it as soon as possible. I have scheduled a meeting with you during your office hours on Friday, September 17th, to go over the material that was covered in class and to ask any questions that I may have.

Please let me know if there are any additional steps that I can take to stay on track with the course or if there are any assignments that I need to submit remotely during my absence.

Thank you for your understanding.

Sincerely,
[Your name]

37. Complaint about a delayed flight

In about 200 words, write an email to the airline company to complain about a delayed flight. Your message must include the following points:

1- Your flight details and date of travel.
2- The reason for your complaint.
3- The consequences of the delay for you.
4- The action you expect the airline to take.

Response:

Dear Sir/Madam,

I am writing to express my disappointment regarding my flight from Toronto to Vancouver on July 15th, 2022, which was delayed by 6 hours.

As a result of the delay, I missed my connecting flight to Victoria and had to spend the night at a hotel, which was not only inconvenient but also costly. Furthermore, I had an important business meeting the next morning in Victoria that I was unable to attend due to the delay, causing me significant financial loss and missed opportunities.

I understand that unforeseen circumstances can arise, but I was disappointed with the lack of communication and assistance from your staff. The departure time was changed several times without any explanation, and the staff seemed unprepared to handle the situation. The lack of information and support made the situation even more frustrating and stressful.

I request that you provide compensation for my expenses incurred due to the delay and the inconvenience caused. I also suggest that the airline provide better communication and support for passengers in the event of such delays in the future.

I appreciate your attention to this matter and hope for a prompt resolution.

Sincerely,
John Doe

38. You recently moved to a new city and need to find a job. Write an email to your friend asking for a reference for a job you're applying for.

In about 200 words, write an email to a friend who is familiar with your work experience, skills, and character, and request that they provide a reference for a job you're applying for. Your message should include the following points:

1- Your current situation, including the city you're living in and the types of jobs you're looking for.
2- The name of the company you're applying to and the position you're seeking.
3- A brief summary of why you're qualified for the job.
4- A request for your friend to provide a reference and any additional information they might need.

Response:

Dear Jane,

I hope this email finds you well. As you know, I recently moved to Toronto, and I'm currently searching for a new job. I'm interested in positions related to marketing, particularly in the areas of branding and communications.

I'm writing to request a reference from you for a job I'm applying for. The company is called XYZ Inc., and they are looking for a Marketing Coordinator to join their team. I believe I would be a great fit for this position because of my experience in branding and communications, as well as my strong writing and analytical skills. I also have experience working with social media platforms, which I understand is an important aspect of the job.

I would be grateful if you could provide a reference for me. If you need any additional information, please let me know, and I'll be happy to send you my resume and cover letter. Please let me know if you have any questions or if there is anything else I can provide.

Thank you so much for your help.

Best regards,

Tom

39. A Lost Item

In about 200 words, write an email to your boss explaining that you have lost an important item, such as a laptop or phone. Your message must include the following points:

1- Introduction and explanation of the situation.
2- The importance of the lost item.
3- Where do you think the item might be.
4- Any actions you have taken to try to find it.
5- Your plan for ensuring this does not happen again.

Response:

Dear Mr. Johnson,

I'm writing to inform you that I've lost my company-issued laptop, and I am quite distressed by the situation. I have searched high and low for it, but it seems to have disappeared entirely. I apologize for any inconvenience this has caused and understand the gravity of this issue.

The laptop was important to me because it contained all my work files, contacts, and project details. It is an essential tool in my daily work routine, and I cannot function without it. Losing the laptop has caused me great inconvenience and I understand it is important to the company as well.

I believe I may have left it on the train during my morning commute. I contacted the lost and found department and filled out a form, but they haven't called me back yet. I will continue to check with them every day until I hear back about the laptop.

To ensure this situation does not happen again, I will keep a closer eye on my belongings and make sure to keep my laptop secured in my bag when traveling. I understand the seriousness of this issue and appreciate your understanding and support.

Sincerely,

Jane Doe

40. Requesting a leave of absence

In about 200 words, write an email to your supervisor requesting a leave of absence. Your message must include the following points:

1- The dates you need to take off.
2- The reason for your leave.
3- How your work will be covered during your absence.
4- Your contact information.

Response:

Dear Mr. Johnson,

I am writing to request a leave of absence from work for two weeks, starting on June 1st, 2023, until June 14th, 2023. The reason for my leave is that my wife and I will be travelling to Europe to visit my parents who live there. They have been experiencing some health issues and we need to be there to provide support and assistance.

During my absence, I will make sure that all of my responsibilities are covered. I have already discussed this with my colleagues and they have agreed to take on my work while I am away. I will provide them with detailed instructions and information on any ongoing projects and ensure that they are fully prepared to take over my duties.

Please let me know if there are any further steps I need to take in order to arrange my leave. I will make sure to be available by phone and email should any urgent issues arise. Thank you for considering my request.

Sincerely,
John Smith
johnsmith@email.com
(123) 456-7890

41. You recently ordered a product online, but when you received it, the item was damaged.

In about 200 words, write an email to the customer service department of the company where you ordered the product. Explain the situation and request a replacement or refund. Your message must include the following points:

1- Details of the order (order number, product name, date of purchase).
2- Description of the damage.
3- Request for a replacement or refund.
4- Contact information.

Response:

Dear Customer Service Team,

I am writing to report that the product I ordered from your online store arrived in damaged condition. The product in question is a 14-inch laptop with order number 123456, purchased on March 15, 2023.

When I received the package on March 18, 2023, I immediately noticed that the laptop box was dented and crushed on one corner. Upon opening the package, I found that the laptop screen was cracked and unusable. The damage was clearly caused by mishandling during shipment.

I am requesting a replacement laptop of the same make and model, as I still need it for work. Alternatively, I would accept a full refund for the purchase price of $999.99. I have attached photos of the damaged product as evidence.

Please let me know what the next steps are to resolve this issue. I can be reached at the email address and phone number provided in my account information. Thank you for your attention to this matter.

Sincerely,
John Doe

42. Request for Volunteer Opportunity

In about 200 words, write an email to the director of a local charity organization to request a volunteer opportunity. Your message should include the following points:

1- Introduction of yourself and your interest in volunteering.
2- Your availability and the type of volunteer work you are interested in.
3- Any relevant experience or skills you can bring to the organization.
4- A request for further information on the volunteer opportunity.

Response:

Dear Mr. Jones,

I hope this email finds you in good health and spirits. My name is Sarah and I am a recent graduate from the University of Toronto. I am excited to begin my career in the non-profit sector and I am interested in volunteering for your organization.

I have some time available during the weekdays and weekends, and I am hoping to contribute my time to a meaningful cause. I am particularly interested in working with the local community and with children, so any opportunity to support these areas would be ideal.

While I do not have direct experience in the non-profit sector, I have volunteered at summer camps, elementary schools, and youth organizations in the past. These experiences have given me an understanding of the challenges that non-profit organizations face and the importance of community support. I am a fast learner and a dedicated worker, and I am eager to apply my skills to help make a positive impact.

If there are any volunteer opportunities available with your organization, I would be grateful if you could provide me with more information. I look forward to hearing back from you soon.

Sincerely,
Sarah

43. Writing a Letter of Complaint to a Restaurant Manager.

In about 200 words, write a letter to the manager of a restaurant to complain about a recent unpleasant experience you had at their establishment. Your message must include:

1- The details of your experience and what specifically went wrong.
2- The impact this experience had on your visit and how it made you feel.
3- Suggestions for how the restaurant can improve to prevent future incidents.
4- A request for compensation or resolution to make up for your bad experience.

Response:

Dear Restaurant Manager,

I recently visited your establishment on Friday evening for a family dinner, and I must say that my experience was not at all pleasant. I am writing to express my disappointment and frustration with the service we received.

To begin with, our food order took over an hour to arrive at our table, and when it did, it was not what we had ordered. The staff was not accommodating when we pointed out the error, and instead, they were quite dismissive of our concerns. Additionally, our drinks were not refilled, and we had to flag down the server to request more water.

The lack of attention to detail and disregard for our satisfaction left a sour taste in our mouths, and it made us feel unwelcome and undervalued as customers. We had been looking forward to this dinner, but the experience was far from enjoyable.

To prevent future incidents, I suggest that your staff undergoes better training in customer service and attention to detail. Additionally, implementing regular checks on food orders and refilling drinks without the need for customers to ask would go a long way in enhancing the dining experience.

As a resolution, I request that the cost of our meal be refunded or a complimentary meal be offered on our next visit. I hope that you take our feedback into consideration and take appropriate measures to improve your services.

Sincerely,
John Doe

44. You recently attended a wedding and received a gift from the bride and groom.

In about 200 words, write a thank-you letter to the couple. Your letter must include the following points:

1- An expression of gratitude for the gift.
2- A description of how you will use the gift.
3- A mention of the wedding ceremony and reception.
4- A closing statement.

Response:

Dear Sarah and David,

I am writing to express my sincere gratitude for the beautiful wedding gift you gave me. Your thoughtfulness and generosity truly touched my heart.

I can't wait to use the elegant crystal vase you gave me. I plan to display it in my living room and fill it with fresh flowers. Every time I look at it, I will think of the wonderful memories from your special day.

The wedding ceremony was simply breathtaking. The bride looked stunning in her gown, and the groom was so dashing in his suit. The reception was a blast, and the food was absolutely delicious. I had so much fun dancing the night away with you both and the other guests.

Thank you again for including me in your special day and for your generous gift. I hope to see you both soon.

With warm regards,
Emily

45. Writing a Complaint Letter to a Store Manager.

In about 200 words, write a letter of complaint to the manager of a store where you recently purchased a faulty product. Your letter should include the following points:

1- Introduce yourself and explain the situation.
2- Describe the product and the issue you are having with it.
3- Explain what steps you have already taken to address the issue.
4- Request a resolution to the problem and express your dissatisfaction with the situation.

Response:

Dear Manager,

My name is Jane Doe, and I am writing to express my disappointment with the faulty product I recently purchased from your store on Main Street. I am hoping you can assist me in resolving this issue.

I purchased a toaster oven from your store a week ago, and upon using it for the first time, I noticed that the top heating element was not working. This defect has made it impossible for me to cook anything properly, and I am extremely disappointed with the quality of the product.

I contacted the customer service department, and they advised me to bring the toaster oven back to the store for a refund or exchange. However, I live quite far from your location, and this is quite an inconvenience for me.

I would appreciate it if you could provide me with a solution that does not require me to make the trip back to the store. Can you provide me with a replacement toaster oven or a refund via mail?

I am disappointed with the quality of the product, and I hope that you can help me in resolving this issue. I look forward to your prompt response.

Sincerely,
Jane Doe

46. You have recently attended a business conference and heard a presentation that you found very informative.

In about 200 words, write an email to the presenter to express your appreciation and highlight the key points that you found most useful. Your message must include the following points:

1- An introduction to yourself and your position.
2- A thank you for the presenter's time and effort.
3- The key points that you found most informative and how you plan to use them.
4- A closing remark.

Response:

Dear Mr. Johnson,

I am writing to express my sincere appreciation for the informative presentation you delivered at the recent business conference in Toronto. My name is Sarah Kim and I am the marketing manager at XYZ Corporation.

Your presentation on "Effective Marketing Strategies in the Digital Age" was truly inspiring and I found it to be one of the most informative sessions at the conference. Your insights into the use of social media platforms for targeted advertising were particularly enlightening, and I plan to incorporate these strategies into our upcoming marketing campaigns. I also appreciated your emphasis on the importance of customer engagement and how it can be achieved through personalized messaging.

Your presentation has given me a fresh perspective on marketing in the digital age and I am confident that the strategies you presented will yield significant benefits for our company.

Once again, thank you for taking the time and effort to share your knowledge and expertise with us. I look forward to future opportunities to learn from you.

Best regards,
Sarah Kim

47. You have received a letter from the editor of a magazine. They have seen a blog post that you wrote and would like to publish it in their upcoming issue.

In about 200 words, write an email response to the editor accepting their offer. Your message must include the following points:

1- Express gratitude for the editor's interest in your work.
2- Confirm that you would like your blog post to be published in the magazine.
3- Request any necessary details from the editor, such as the deadline for submitting the article, the word count limit, or any other requirements.
4- Mention that you are open to making any edits or revisions that the editor suggests.

Response:

Dear Editor,

I am honored and grateful to have received your letter expressing interest in publishing my blog post, "The Benefits of Mindful Meditation," in your upcoming magazine issue. It means so much to me that my writing resonated with you and your readers.

I am thrilled to accept your offer to have my work featured in your esteemed publication. It would be an incredible opportunity for me to reach a wider audience and share my passion for mindfulness with others.

If it's not too much trouble, could you please provide me with the deadline for submitting the article and any word count limitations or other requirements? I want to make sure that I meet all the necessary criteria for publication.

Additionally, I am open to any suggestions or edits you may have regarding my post. I want to ensure that it is the best version possible and is well-suited for your publication.

Thank you again for considering my work. I look forward to working with you and your team on this exciting project.

Best regards,

[Your Name]

48. You recently read an article about a local community garden that is looking for volunteers.

In about 200 words, write an email to the organizer expressing your interest in volunteering. Your message must include the following points:

1- Your introduction and how you found out about the community garden.
2- Why you are interested in volunteering.
3- The amount of time you are available to volunteer.
4- Any previous experience you have with gardening or community service.

Response:

Dear Community Garden Organizer,

I recently came across an article about your local community garden and was excited to learn about the work you are doing to promote sustainable and healthy living. I am writing to express my interest in volunteering with your organization.

I have always been passionate about gardening and believe that it is an important way to connect with nature and promote environmental sustainability. I am especially drawn to community gardens because they provide a space for people to come together and work towards a common goal.

As for my availability, I am currently working part-time and have some free time during the week and on weekends. I would be happy to commit a few hours a week to help maintain the garden and assist with any other tasks that need to be done.

In terms of experience, I have worked on several gardening projects in the past, both independently and with community organizations. I have experience with planting, weeding, and harvesting, as well as basic maintenance tasks like watering and fertilizing.

I look forward to the opportunity to work with you and contribute to the success of your community garden. Thank you for your consideration.

Best regards,
Jane Doe

49. You are a customer who ordered a product online, but the product has not arrived on time.

In about 200 words, write an email to the company explaining the situation and requesting information about the status of your order. Your message must include the following points:

1- An introduction and explanation of the situation.
2- The date the product was supposed to arrive.
3- A request for information on the status of the order.
4- A polite but firm request for compensation if the product does not arrive soon.

Response:

Dear Customer Service,

I am writing to inquire about the status of my recent order for a pair of running shoes. I placed the order on your website on April 1st, and was informed that the shoes would arrive by April 10th, but it has now been over a week since that date and the shoes have not yet arrived.

As an avid runner, I was counting on these shoes for my upcoming half marathon. However, due to the delay in the delivery, I am now left without the necessary footwear for the race, which is very disappointing.

I would appreciate if you could provide me with any information regarding the status of my order. Have the shoes been shipped, and if so, what is the expected delivery date? If they have not been shipped, could you please let me know when they will be dispatched?

Additionally, I would like to request compensation for the inconvenience caused by the delay. I understand that sometimes delivery issues may arise, but I am hoping that your company can make things right by offering a discount on a future purchase or some other form of compensation.

Thank you for your attention to this matter. I look forward to hearing from you soon.

Sincerely,
[Your Name]

50. You recently moved to a new neighborhood and you are having trouble with your neighbors who have loud parties late at night.

In about 200 words, write an email to your landlord explaining the problem and asking for assistance. Your message must include the following points:

1- Introduction to the problem
2- How the parties are affecting you
3- Request for assistance
4- Suggestion for a possible solution

Response:

Dear [Landlord's name],

I am writing to bring to your attention a problem that has been affecting my ability to live comfortably in my new apartment. I have recently moved into this neighborhood and my neighbors in the apartment across the hall have been throwing loud parties late into the night. I understand that social gatherings are part of life, but the noise level has been excessive and disruptive.

These parties have been affecting my ability to sleep at night and have been disrupting my daily routines. I have been experiencing fatigue and lack of focus during the day due to the lack of sleep. I have tried speaking with my neighbors to request that they lower the noise levels, but it has not resulted in any changes.

I would greatly appreciate your assistance in resolving this issue. Could you please speak to my neighbors and remind them of the apartment complex's noise policy? I suggest that we also post reminders in the common areas to remind residents of the policy and the importance of being considerate of their neighbors.

Thank you for your attention to this matter. I look forward to hearing from you.

Sincerely,
[Your name]

CELPIP Writing Task 2: Essay

51- Working from Home or Working from the Office?

Your company is considering allowing employees to work from home permanently. Some employees are excited about the prospect of no longer commuting and having more flexibility in their work schedules. Others are concerned about feeling isolated and missing out on the social aspects of working in an office. The HR department has asked for your opinion.

1- Choose the option that you prefer.
2- Why do you prefer your choice?
3- Explain the reasons for your choice.
4- Write about 150-200 words.

Option A: I prefer to work from home permanently.
Option B: I prefer to work from the office permanently.

Response:

I am in favor of working from home permanently.

Firstly, working from home eliminates the daily commute, which is often stressful and time-consuming. This allows me to use the extra time to be more productive at work and attend to personal matters. Additionally, working from home provides me with a comfortable and familiar environment, which helps to reduce stress levels and increase job satisfaction.

Secondly, I believe that working from home increases work-life balance, which in turn improves employee productivity and morale. It allows me to have more flexibility in my schedule, which helps me better manage both personal and work-related tasks. This freedom also allows me to work during my most productive hours, which can lead to better quality work.

Lastly, with the availability of modern technology, working from home has become an easy and efficient way to communicate with colleagues and clients. Collaboration tools such as video conferencing and project management software allow for effective communication and collaboration, regardless of physical location.

In conclusion, I am fully in favor of working from home permanently. It provides numerous benefits, including reduced stress levels, increased productivity, improved work-life balance, and more efficient communication tools.

52. Public Transportation or Personal Vehicle?

Your city council is considering implementing new policies to encourage the use of public transportation. Some citizens believe that this will reduce traffic congestion and air pollution. Others argue that personal vehicles are more convenient and offer greater flexibility. The city council has asked for your opinion.

1- Choose the option that you prefer.
2- Why do you prefer your choice?
3- Explain the reasons for your choice.
4- Write about 150-200 words.

Option A: I prefer using public transportation.
Option B: I prefer using a personal vehicle.

Response:

I prefer using public transportation over a personal vehicle.

Firstly, using public transportation reduces traffic congestion, which is a major problem in most cities. Public transportation reduces the number of cars on the road, which leads to fewer traffic jams and less time spent in traffic. It also makes the roads safer, as there are fewer accidents and less road rage.

Secondly, using public transportation reduces air pollution. Cars emit pollutants that harm the environment, and public transportation produces far less pollution per person than personal vehicles. Using public transportation is also more energy-efficient, as a single bus can carry dozens of passengers, reducing the amount of fuel needed to transport each person.

Thirdly, using public transportation can save money. Personal vehicles are expensive to maintain and require fuel, parking fees, and other expenses. Public transportation is more affordable, especially if discounted passes or monthly subscriptions are available.

Lastly, using public transportation can be a more pleasant experience than driving. Public transportation allows you to relax, read a book, or listen to music while traveling. It can also be an opportunity to socialize with other people.

In conclusion, I strongly believe that using public transportation is a better option than using a personal vehicle. It reduces traffic congestion, air pollution, and costs, while also providing a more pleasant and relaxing travel experience.

53. Online Shopping or Traditional Shopping?

Online shopping has become increasingly popular in recent years. Some people prefer the convenience and ease of shopping from home, while others enjoy the social aspect of traditional shopping in a physical store. Your friend has asked for your opinion on this matter.

1- Choose the option that you prefer.
2- Why do you prefer your choice?
3- Explain the reasons for your choice.
4- Write about 150-200 words.

Option A: I prefer online shopping.
Option B: I prefer traditional shopping.

Response:

I prefer online shopping over traditional shopping.

Firstly, online shopping provides convenience and saves time. With just a few clicks, I can easily find the products I want and have them delivered directly to my doorstep. I do not have to worry about finding parking, navigating through crowded stores, or carrying heavy shopping bags. This saves me time and effort, which I can use for other activities.

Secondly, online shopping provides a wider range of products and prices. Physical stores may not always carry the exact item I am looking for, but online stores have a much larger inventory, which increases my chances of finding the right product. Additionally, online stores often offer better prices due to lower overhead costs and more competition.

Thirdly, online shopping allows for greater flexibility in payment options. I can pay for my purchases with a variety of payment methods, including credit cards, debit cards, and online payment platforms. This allows me to choose the payment method that is most convenient for me.

Lastly, online shopping is safer and more secure than ever before. Most online retailers use encryption technology to protect personal and financial information. They also offer secure payment methods and easy returns policies, which gives me peace of mind when making purchases online.

In conclusion, I strongly prefer online shopping over traditional shopping. It provides convenience, wider product options, better prices, greater payment flexibility, and safety and security.

54. Living in a Big City or Living in a Small Town?

Many people debate whether it is better to live in a big city or a small town. Your friend is moving and is unsure about which type of place to choose. Your friend has asked for your opinion, and you must write a response.

1- Choose the option that you prefer.
2- Why do you prefer your choice?
3- Explain the reasons for your choice.
4- Write about 150-200 words.

Option A: I prefer living in a big city.
Option B: I prefer living in a small town.

Response:

I prefer living in a big city over living in a small town.

Firstly, big cities offer more job opportunities and higher salaries. There are more businesses and industries in big cities, which means there are more jobs available. The job market is also more diverse, with opportunities in different fields and industries. The salaries are often higher in big cities due to the higher cost of living, which means you can earn more and have a better standard of living.

Secondly, big cities offer more cultural and entertainment options. There are more museums, theaters, concerts, and other events in big cities, which means there is always something to do. The nightlife in big cities is also more vibrant, with many restaurants, bars, and clubs to choose from. The diverse population in big cities also means there are more opportunities to experience different cultures and cuisines.

Thirdly, big cities offer more convenience and accessibility. Public transportation is more extensive and efficient in big cities, which means you can get around easily without a car. There are also more amenities, such as supermarkets, shops, and services, which means you can get everything you need without having to travel far.

In conclusion, I prefer living in a big city over living in a small town. Big cities offer more job opportunities and higher salaries, more cultural and entertainment options, and more convenience and accessibility. However, I understand that living in a small town can offer a more peaceful and close-knit community, and may be preferable for some people.

55. Work Schedule Preferences

Your company is considering changing the work schedule for employees in your department. They have proposed two options for the new schedule and want your input on which option you prefer.

Option A: Work Monday to Friday from 8:00 AM to 4:00 PM with a 30-minute lunch break.
Option B: Work Monday to Thursday from 7:00 AM to 6:00 PM with a 1-hour lunch break, and have Fridays off.

1- Choose the option that you prefer.
2- Why do you prefer your choice?
3- Explain the reasons for your choice.
4- Write about 150-200 words.

Response:

Thank you for considering the opinions of the employees regarding the proposed new work schedule. After reviewing the options presented, I prefer option B - working from Monday to Thursday with a longer workday and having Fridays off.

First and foremost, the extra day off will allow me to pursue personal interests and commitments that I have had to neglect due to my current work schedule. This will not only lead to greater job satisfaction, but also improved work-life balance. Furthermore, having Fridays off will also allow me to schedule appointments and errands that are typically only available during regular business hours.

Moreover, the longer workdays from Monday to Thursday will allow me to complete my work with more focus and fewer distractions. The one-hour lunch break will provide ample time to relax and recharge, which will in turn help me be more productive during the remainder of the day.

Overall, I believe that option B will lead to greater employee satisfaction and productivity, and I hope that you will consider implementing this schedule for our department.

56. Company Benefits

Your company is considering adding a new benefit for employees. They have proposed two options and want your input on which option you prefer.

Option A: Free gym membership for all employees.
Option B: A company-sponsored volunteer day where employees can choose to participate in a community service project during work hours.

1- Choose the option that you prefer.
2- Why do you prefer your choice?
3- Explain the reasons for your choice.
4- Write about 150-200 words.

Response:

I believe that option B - a company-sponsored volunteer day - would be the most beneficial for both the employees and the community.

Volunteering is an excellent way for employees to give back to the community and feel a sense of purpose beyond their work responsibilities. The opportunity to participate in a community service project during work hours would provide employees with a much-needed break from their routine work and help them connect with their community. It would also help to boost employee morale and job satisfaction.

Moreover, the company would benefit from the positive publicity and reputation that comes with supporting the community. It would also be a great team-building activity, as employees from different departments can work together towards a common goal. This can ultimately lead to better communication and collaboration within the workplace.

While a free gym membership is also a valuable benefit, I believe that it only benefits those who are already interested in exercising. On the other hand, a company-sponsored volunteer day would benefit both the community and the employees, regardless of their individual interests.

Thank you for considering our feedback, and I hope that you will consider implementing the company-sponsored volunteer day.

57. Office Space

Your company is considering a move to a new location. They have proposed two options for the new office space and want your input on which option you prefer.

Option A: A larger office space in the suburbs with ample parking.
Option B: A smaller office space in the city center with limited parking.

1- Choose the option that you prefer.
2- Why do you prefer your choice?
3- Explain the reasons for your choice.
4- Write about 150-200 words.

Response:

Thank you for considering the input of employees in the decision-making process for the new office location. After careful consideration, I prefer option B - a smaller office space in the city center, despite the limited parking.

The location of the office is crucial for many employees, as it can significantly impact their commute time and transportation costs. A smaller office space in the city center would be more convenient for employees who rely on public transportation or live within the city limits. It would also provide more opportunities for lunch options and entertainment during breaks, which can contribute to employee satisfaction.

Moreover, a smaller office space would encourage employees to collaborate and communicate with each other more effectively. This would lead to better teamwork, and a more cohesive work environment. In addition, the limited parking would encourage employees to use public transportation, which is better for the environment.

While a larger office space in the suburbs may provide more

space, ample parking, and potentially lower rent, it would be less convenient for many employees. The time and money saved on transportation would likely offset any potential rent savings. Furthermore, a smaller office space can be more efficient, as it forces employees to be more organized and avoid clutter.

In conclusion, a smaller office space in the city center would be more convenient, environmentally-friendly, and efficient, and I hope that you will consider this option for the new office location.

58. Workplace Attire

Your company is considering implementing a new dress code policy. They have proposed two options for the dress code and want your input on which option you prefer.

Option A: Business formal attire (suits, ties, dresses, skirts) for all employees.
Option B: Business casual attire (khakis, collared shirts, blouses, skirts) for all employees.

1- Choose the option that you prefer.
2- Why do you prefer your choice?
3- Explain the reasons for your choice.
4- Write about 150-200 words.

Response:

Dear Management Team,

I appreciate the opportunity to provide my input on the proposed dress code policy. After careful consideration, I believe that option B - business casual attire - would be the most appropriate dress code policy for our company.

Business casual attire is a comfortable and practical dress code for employees, especially those who work in a professional environment. It strikes a balance between professional and casual attire, which can help to improve employee morale and productivity. The flexibility in attire allows employees to feel more relaxed and comfortable in their work environment.

Moreover, business casual attire is more affordable and accessible for employees than business formal attire. It can reduce the financial burden on employees, as they don't have to spend a lot of money on expensive suits or dresses. This can lead to better employee satisfaction and retention.

On the other hand, a business formal dress code policy can

be uncomfortable and impractical for some employees. It can create a stressful work environment, as employees may feel pressured to conform to a strict dress code. It can also be difficult to enforce, as it can be challenging to define what constitutes "business formal attire".

In conclusion, I believe that a business casual dress code policy would be the most appropriate for our company. It is a practical, comfortable, and affordable option for employees, and it can improve overall employee morale and productivity.

59. Healthy Lunch Options

Your company is considering implementing a new healthy lunch options program. They have proposed two options for the program and want your input on which option you prefer.

Option A: Offering a weekly salad bar with a variety of toppings, including grilled chicken, tofu, and mixed vegetables.
Option B: Offering a weekly sandwich bar with a variety of whole-grain bread, deli meats, cheeses, and vegetables.

1- Choose the option that you prefer.
2- Why do you prefer your choice?
3- Explain the reasons for your choice.
4- Write about 150-200 words.

Response:

Dear Management Team,

Thank you for considering my input on the proposed healthy lunch options program. After careful consideration, I believe that option A - a weekly salad bar - would be the most appropriate option for our company.

Offering a salad bar with a variety of toppings, including grilled chicken, tofu, and mixed vegetables, is a healthy and nutritious option for employees. Salads are an excellent source of vitamins and minerals and can be a great way to promote a healthy lifestyle. They are also versatile and can be customized to meet the dietary needs and preferences of individual employees.

Moreover, salads are a great option for employees who are trying to watch their calorie intake. Sandwiches, on the other hand, can be high in calories, especially if they are made with white bread and high-fat deli meats and cheeses. A salad bar can provide a low-calorie option for employees who are trying to maintain a healthy weight or lose weight.

Finally, offering a salad bar can help to promote a sense of community and teamwork among employees. Employees can bond over shared healthy food choices and can support each other in making healthy lifestyle choices. This can lead to better teamwork, collaboration, and overall job satisfaction.

In conclusion, I believe that a weekly salad bar would be the most appropriate option for our company's healthy lunch options program. It is a healthy, nutritious, and customizable option that can help to promote a sense of community and teamwork among employees.

60. Workplace Flexibility

Your company is considering introducing a new workplace flexibility policy. They have proposed two options for the policy and want your input on which option you prefer.

Option A: Allowing employees to work from home one day per week.
Option B: Allowing employees to choose their own work hours, as long as they complete their work within the standard workweek.

1- Choose the option that you prefer.
2- Why do you prefer your choice?
3- Explain the reasons for your choice.

Response:

I appreciate the opportunity to provide input on the proposed workplace flexibility policy. After careful consideration, I believe that option B - allowing employees to choose their own work hours - would be the most appropriate option for our company.

Allowing employees to choose their own work hours can be highly beneficial for both employees and the company. It can increase job satisfaction and employee engagement, as employees feel trusted and empowered to manage their own work schedules. It can also lead to higher productivity, as employees can work during their most productive hours, whether that is early in the morning, late at night, or during the traditional workday.

Furthermore, this option can help to reduce employee stress and improve work-life balance. Employees can schedule their work hours around their personal lives, such as appointments or childcare responsibilities, which can reduce stress and increase overall job satisfaction. Additionally, it can reduce absenteeism and turnover rates, as employees are more likely to stay with a company that offers a flexible work schedule.

On the other hand, option A, allowing employees to work from home one day per week, can be limiting and may not provide the level of flexibility that employees need. It can also lead to communication challenges and a lack of team cohesion, as employees may feel disconnected from their colleagues and the workplace.

In conclusion, I believe that option B - allowing employees to choose their own work hours - would be the most appropriate option for our company's workplace flexibility policy. It can lead to higher productivity, job satisfaction, and work-life balance for employees, while also reducing absenteeism and turnover rates for the company.

61. Health and Fitness Programs

Your company is considering introducing a new health and fitness program for employees. They have proposed two options for the program and want your input on which option you prefer.

Option A: Offering healthy snacks and drinks in the office cafeteria.
Option B: Providing a free gym membership to employees.

1- Choose the option that you prefer.
2- Why do you prefer your choice?
3- Explain the reasons for your choice.

Response:

Thank you for considering input on the proposed health and fitness program. After considering both options, I believe that option B - providing a free gym membership to employees - would be the most appropriate option for our company.

Offering a free gym membership can be highly beneficial for both employees and the company. It can improve employee health and wellness, which can lead to lower healthcare costs and reduced absenteeism rates. Furthermore, it can improve employee morale and job satisfaction, as employees feel valued and supported by the company.

In contrast, option A, offering healthy snacks and drinks in the office cafeteria, may not provide the same level of benefits as a gym membership. While providing healthy snacks and drinks can encourage healthy eating habits, it may not address the need for regular exercise, which is essential for maintaining good health and wellness.

Moreover, a gym membership can be more inclusive, accommodating the needs of all employees. Not everyone may be able to benefit from healthy snacks and drinks, but a gym membership can benefit employees of all ages and fitness levels. It can also provide an opportunity for employees to socialize and build relationships with colleagues outside of the office, which can lead to increased team cohesion and a positive workplace culture.

In conclusion, I believe that option B - providing a free gym membership to employees - would be the most appropriate option for our company's health and fitness program. It can lead to improved employee health and wellness, lower healthcare costs, and increased job satisfaction, while also promoting team cohesion and a positive workplace culture.

62. Renewable Energy

Your town council is considering two proposals for a new renewable energy project to reduce the town's carbon footprint. They want your input on which option you prefer.

Option A: Install a large solar panel array in a nearby field to generate electricity for the town.
Option B: Build a wind farm on a nearby hill to generate electricity for the town.

1- Choose the option that you prefer.
2- Why do you prefer your choice?
3- Explain the reasons for your choice.

Response:

Thank you for the opportunity to provide input on the proposed renewable energy project. After careful consideration, I believe that option B - building a wind farm on a nearby hill to generate electricity for the town - would be the most appropriate option for our community.

Firstly, wind farms have been shown to be more efficient than solar panels in generating electricity. They can produce electricity even on cloudy days, and can generate electricity at night, when solar panels are not able to produce energy. This means that a wind farm would be a more reliable source of renewable energy for our town.

Secondly, wind farms have a smaller environmental footprint compared to solar panels. Solar panels require a significant amount of land to generate the same amount of electricity as a wind farm. Additionally, wind farms are more aesthetically pleasing than large solar panel arrays, and can even attract tourism to the area.

Lastly, building a wind farm would provide an opportunity for our town to create new jobs and stimulate economic growth.

Wind farms require engineers, technicians, and other skilled workers to design, construct, and maintain the turbines. This can lead to job creation and increased economic activity in our community.

In contrast, while option A may provide a local source of renewable energy, it may not be as efficient or reliable as a wind farm. Additionally, it may require a larger land area, and may not provide the same economic benefits as building a wind farm.

In conclusion, I believe that option B - building a wind farm on a nearby hill to generate electricity for the town - would be the most appropriate option for our community. It can provide a reliable source of renewable energy, has a smaller environmental footprint than solar panels, and can create new jobs and stimulate economic growth in our community.

63. Public Transportation

Your city is considering investing in either a new subway system or an expansion of the existing bus network. They want your input on which option you prefer.

Option A: Build a new subway system.
Option B: Expand the existing bus network.

1- Choose the option that you prefer.
2- Why do you prefer your choice?
3- Explain the reasons for your choice.

Response:

After careful consideration, I believe that option B, expanding the existing bus network, would be the most appropriate option for our city.

Firstly, expanding the existing bus network would be a more cost-effective option compared to building a new subway system. The construction of a new subway system would require a significant amount of investment in both time and money, whereas expanding the bus network would require less initial investment and could be implemented more quickly. This would make it a more practical and efficient solution for our city's transportation needs.

Secondly, expanding the existing bus network would have a broader impact on the community as it would provide transportation to a wider area. Buses have greater flexibility to serve more neighborhoods and can be rerouted easily to accommodate changes in traffic and commuting patterns. This would be especially beneficial for commuters who live in areas that are not served by the current subway system or are too far from the subway stations.

Lastly, expanding the existing bus network would be more environmentally friendly compared to building a new subway system. While subway systems have a reputation for being environmentally friendly, they require significant resources to construct, including mining for materials and transporting them to the construction site. In contrast, expanding the existing bus network would have a much smaller environmental impact.

In conclusion, I believe that expanding the existing bus network would be the most appropriate investment for our city. It would be a more cost-effective and practical solution that would benefit a wider range of commuters and have a smaller environmental impact. Thank you for considering my input.

64. Fast Food vs. Home-Cooked Meals

Your friend is trying to decide whether to continue eating fast food or start cooking meals at home. They want your opinion on which option is better.

Option A: Continue eating fast food.
Option B: Start cooking meals at home.

1- Choose the option that you prefer.
2- Why do you prefer your choice?
3- Explain the reasons for your choice.

Response:

I am writing to provide my opinion on whether to continue eating fast food or start cooking meals at home. After careful consideration, I believe that option B, starting to cook meals at home, would be the better option.

Firstly, cooking meals at home would be healthier than eating fast food. Fast food is often high in calories, saturated fats, and sodium, which can lead to obesity, heart disease, and other health problems. By cooking meals at home, you can control the ingredients and cooking methods to ensure that they are healthy and nutritious.

Secondly, cooking meals at home would be more cost-effective than eating fast food. Fast food can be expensive, especially if you eat it frequently. By cooking meals at home, you can save money on groceries and avoid the added costs of dining out or ordering in.

Lastly, cooking meals at home would be more enjoyable than eating fast food. Cooking can be a fun and creative activity that allows you to experiment with different flavours and cuisines. It can also be a great way to bond with family and friends, and to develop new culinary skills.

In conclusion, I believe that starting to cook meals at home would be the better option for you. It would be healthier, more cost-effective, and more enjoyable than eating fast food. I hope that you find this advice helpful in making your decision.

65. Online Shopping vs. In-Store Shopping

Many people prefer online shopping to in-store shopping. Others argue that in-store shopping is still preferable. Which do you think is better?

Option A: Online shopping is better.
Option B: In-store shopping is better.

1- Choose the option that you prefer.
2- Why do you prefer your choice?
3- Explain the reasons for your choice.

Response:

In my opinion, online shopping is better than in-store shopping for several reasons.

Firstly, online shopping is more convenient. You can shop from the comfort of your own home without having to travel to a physical store. This saves time and effort, especially for people who have busy schedules or live far away from shopping centers.

Secondly, online shopping offers a wider range of products. Physical stores are limited by their physical space and inventory, but online stores have a much larger selection of products available. This means that you can find exactly what you are looking for without having to visit multiple stores.

Thirdly, online shopping often offers better prices and deals than in-store shopping. Online retailers can offer lower prices because they don't have the overhead costs of maintaining a physical store. They also frequently offer special discounts and promotions, which can save you even more money.

Lastly, online shopping is safer during a pandemic or other health crisis. You can avoid the crowds and minimize the risk of infection by shopping online instead of going to a physical store.

In conclusion, I believe that online shopping is the better option.

It is more convenient, offers a wider range of products, often has better prices, and is safer during a pandemic. While in-store shopping may offer some advantages, I believe that online shopping is the better choice for most people.

66. Social Media: Positive or Negative Impact?

Social media has become a prominent part of our daily lives. Some people argue that it has a positive impact, while others argue that it has a negative impact. Which do you think is true?

Option A: Social media has a positive impact.
Option B: Social media has a negative impact.

1- Choose the option that you prefer.
2- Why do you prefer your choice?
3- Explain the reasons for your choice.

Response:

In my opinion, social media has a negative impact on our lives, despite its popularity and widespread use.

Firstly, social media can be addictive and time-consuming. It is easy to get sucked into scrolling through your feeds for hours on end, which can lead to a lack of productivity and even social isolation. This can be particularly problematic for young people who may be more susceptible to addiction and have a greater need for social interaction.

Secondly, social media can be a breeding ground for misinformation and fake news. With so many different voices and opinions being shared on social media, it can be difficult to distinguish between fact and fiction. This can lead to a lack of trust in reliable sources of information and an increase in polarization and division.

Thirdly, social media can negatively impact mental health. Studies have shown that social media use can lead to increased feelings of anxiety, depression, and low self-esteem. This is due in part to the constant pressure to present a perfect image of oneself online, as well as the comparison to others that social media encourages.

Lastly, social media can have a negative impact on privacy and security. With so much personal information being shared online, it can be easy for cybercriminals to gain access to sensitive data. Additionally, social media companies themselves may use user data for targeted advertising and other purposes without the user's knowledge or consent.

In conclusion, while social media may have some positive aspects, such as connecting people and promoting free expression, I believe that its negative impacts are significant and cannot be ignored. Social media addiction, fake news, mental health issues, and privacy concerns all contribute to the overall negative impact of social media on our lives.

67. The Importance of Learning a Second Language

Learning a second language has become increasingly important in today's globalized world. Some people believe that it is crucial to learn a second language, while others argue that it is not necessary. Which do you think is true?

Option A: Learning a second language is crucial.
Option B: Learning a second language is not necessary.

1- Choose the option that you prefer.
2- Why do you prefer your choice?
3- Explain the reasons for your choice.

Response:
In my opinion, learning a second language is crucial in today's globalized world.

Firstly, learning a second language opens up a world of opportunities. In a globalized economy, businesses are looking for employees who are bilingual or multilingual. Knowing a second language can give a job candidate a competitive edge and increase their chances of success.

Secondly, learning a second language can enhance cultural understanding and communication. It can help individuals to connect with people from different cultures and understand their perspectives. This can lead to more meaningful relationships and better communication, both personally and professionally.

Thirdly, learning a second language can improve cognitive abilities. Studies have shown that learning a second language can improve memory, problem-solving skills, and multitasking abilities. It can also delay the onset of age-related cognitive decline and dementia.

Lastly, learning a second language can be a fun and rewarding experience. It can provide a sense of accomplishment and satisfaction, and open up opportunities for travel and cultural exchange.

In conclusion, while some may argue that learning a second language is not necessary, I believe that it is crucial in today's globalized world. The benefits of learning a second language, such as increased job opportunities, cultural understanding, improved cognitive abilities, and personal fulfillment, make it a worthwhile endeavor for anyone.

68. The Benefits and Drawbacks of Social Media

Social media has become an integral part of modern society. While there are many benefits to using social media, there are also drawbacks. In your opinion, which outweighs the other - the benefits or the drawbacks? Provide reasons for your answer.

Option A: The benefits of social media outweigh the drawbacks.
Option B: The drawbacks of social media outweigh the benefits.

Response:

In my opinion, the benefits of social media far outweigh the drawbacks. There are several reasons why I believe this to be true.

First and foremost, social media has revolutionized the way we communicate with each other. It has made it easier than ever to stay in touch with friends and family who live far away, and it has also made it easier to meet new people who share our interests and passions. Social media has brought people together in a way that was not possible before, and this is a truly amazing thing.

Secondly, social media has also made it easier to share information and stay up-to-date with the latest news and events. With the click of a button, we can access information from around the world, and we can also share our own experiences and opinions with others.

While there are certainly some drawbacks to social media, such as the potential for cyberbullying and the spread of fake news, I believe that these are outweighed by the benefits. With proper education and awareness, we can address these issues and continue to enjoy the many benefits that social media has to offer.

Overall, I believe that social media has had a profoundly positive impact on our world, and that its benefits far outweigh its drawbacks.

69. The Advantages and Disadvantages of Online Shopping

Online shopping has become increasingly popular in recent years, and it offers many advantages over traditional shopping. However, there are also some disadvantages to online shopping. In your opinion, which outweighs the other - the advantages or the disadvantages? Provide reasons for your answer.

Option A: The advantages of online shopping outweigh the disadvantages.
Option B: The disadvantages of online shopping outweigh the advantages.

Response:

In my opinion, the advantages of online shopping outweigh the disadvantages. There are several reasons why I believe this to be true.

Firstly, online shopping is incredibly convenient. With just a few clicks, we can purchase almost anything we need, from groceries to clothing to electronics. We no longer have to spend time driving to and from the store, searching for parking, and standing in long checkout lines.

Secondly, online shopping offers a wider variety of products to choose from. We can easily compare prices and read product reviews to make informed purchasing decisions. Additionally, we have access to products from around the world that may not be available in our local stores.

While there are certainly some disadvantages to online shopping, such as the potential for fraud and the inability to physically examine a product before purchasing it, I believe that these are outweighed by the advantages. With proper precautions and common sense, we can mitigate these risks and enjoy the many benefits that online shopping has to offer.

Overall, I believe that online shopping has greatly improved our shopping experience and made our lives easier and more efficient, and that its advantages far outweigh its disadvantages.

70. Should Junk Food Be Banned in Schools?

Many schools around the world have banned the sale of junk food in an effort to promote healthy eating habits among students. However, some argue that it is not necessary to ban junk food in schools. In your opinion, should junk food be banned in schools? Provide reasons for your answer.

Option A: Junk food should be banned in schools.
Option B: Junk food should not be banned in schools.

Response:

I strongly believe that junk food should be banned in schools. There are several reasons why I think this is necessary.

Firstly, junk food is often high in calories, sugar, and fat, and lacks the essential nutrients that growing children need to thrive. By offering healthier options in school cafeterias and vending machines, we can help students develop good eating habits and prevent the development of health problems like obesity and diabetes.

Secondly, studies have shown that consuming junk food can have negative effects on academic performance. Children who eat a diet high in processed foods and sugar are more likely to experience fatigue, poor concentration, and difficulty with memory and learning.

Finally, schools have a responsibility to promote the health and well-being of their students. By providing healthy food options and promoting physical activity, schools can help students develop habits that will benefit them throughout their lives.

While some argue that junk food should not be banned in schools because it is a matter of personal choice, I believe that the health and well-being of students should be the top priority. By banning junk food in schools, we can help students develop healthy habits that will last a lifetime.

71. Should Animals Be Used for Testing New Products?

Animal testing is a controversial issue. While some believe that it is necessary to test new products on animals before they can be released to the public, others argue that it is cruel and unnecessary. In your opinion, should animals be used for testing new products? Provide reasons for your answer.

Option A: Animals should not be used for testing new products.
Option B: Animals should be used for testing new products.

Response:

I strongly believe that animals should not be used for testing new products. There are several reasons why I think this is necessary.

Firstly, animal testing is cruel and inhumane. Animals are subjected to painful and often deadly experiments in the name of science, and many suffer greatly as a result. As a society, we should not tolerate the unnecessary suffering of other living beings.

Secondly, animal testing is not always accurate or reliable. Animals are not the same as humans, and the results of animal tests do not always translate to humans. This means that testing on animals can sometimes give false results, leading to dangerous or ineffective products being released to the public.

Finally, there are alternative methods for testing new products that do not involve animals. These include computer simulations, cell cultures, and human volunteers. While these methods may not be perfect, they are often more accurate and reliable than animal testing.

While some argue that animal testing is necessary to ensure the safety of new products, I believe that the suffering of animals is not worth the potential benefits. By using alternative methods of testing, we can ensure the safety and effectiveness of new products without causing harm to other living beings.

72. Should College Tuition Be Free?

In recent years, there has been growing discussion about the cost of college tuition and whether it should be free. Some argue that higher education is a right and should be accessible to all, regardless of their financial situation. Others argue that free college tuition is not feasible and would have negative consequences. In your opinion, should college tuition be free? Provide reasons for your answer.

Option A: College tuition should not be free.
Option B: College tuition should be free.

Response:

In my opinion, college tuition should be free for all students. There are several reasons why I believe this is necessary.

Firstly, higher education is a right, not a privilege. Everyone should have the opportunity to pursue their dreams and reach their full potential, regardless of their financial situation. Education is key to improving the lives of individuals and society as a whole, and access to higher education should not be limited by economic barriers.

Secondly, free college tuition would reduce the burden of student debt. Many students are forced to take out large loans in order to pay for their education, which can take years or even decades to pay off. By eliminating tuition fees, students would be able to focus on their studies and graduate without the burden of crushing debt.

Finally, free college tuition would benefit society as a whole. A more educated population leads to greater innovation, productivity, and economic growth. By investing in higher education, we can create a more prosperous and equitable society for all.

While some may argue that free college tuition is not feasible, I believe that it is a worthy investment in our future. By ensuring that everyone has access to higher education, we can create a more just and prosperous society for generations to come.

73. Bicycle lanes in the city

Many cities around the world have been adding bicycle lanes to their streets to promote cycling as an alternative mode of transportation. However, some people argue that the space used for these lanes could be better utilized for cars or public transit. Your city is considering adding more bicycle lanes. The city council has asked for public opinion.

Do you support adding more bicycle lanes to the city?
Why or why not?
Explain your reasons for your choice.
Write about 150-200 words.
Option A: Yes, I support adding more bicycle lanes to the city.
Option B: No, I do not support adding more bicycle lanes to the city.

Response:

I am writing to express my support for adding more bicycle lanes to the city. In my opinion, this would be a great step towards making the city more environmentally friendly, healthy, and safe.

Firstly, the addition of bicycle lanes will encourage more people to choose cycling as a mode of transportation, leading to a reduction in air pollution and traffic congestion. This, in turn, will improve the overall quality of life for residents, as well as attracting more tourists to the city.

Secondly, cycling is a great form of exercise, and promoting it will contribute to a healthier population. As a cyclist myself, I have noticed how much easier it is to get around the city on a bike, especially during rush hour traffic.

Finally, bicycle lanes make the streets safer for cyclists and drivers alike. They provide a dedicated space for cyclists, reducing the risk of accidents and injuries. With more bicycle lanes, drivers will also become more accustomed to sharing the road with cyclists, making the streets safer for everyone.

In conclusion, I urge the city council to add more bicycle lanes to the city. This will have a positive impact on the environment, health, and safety of the city's residents.

74. Online Classes vs. Traditional Classes

Due to the ongoing pandemic, many schools and universities have shifted to online classes instead of in-person classes. However, there are still some schools and universities that continue to offer traditional classes. Some people prefer online classes while others prefer traditional classes. What is your preference?

1- Choose the option that you prefer: online classes or traditional classes.
2- Why do you prefer your choice?
3- Explain the reasons for your choice.
4- Write about 150-200 words.

Option A: I prefer online classes.
Option B: I prefer traditional classes.

Response:

I prefer online classes to traditional classes for several reasons. Firstly, online classes offer more flexibility and convenience. As a working professional, I often have a busy schedule and it can be challenging to attend traditional classes regularly. However, with online classes, I can study and complete assignments at my own pace and on my own schedule. This has allowed me to pursue further education without having to sacrifice my work or personal life.

Secondly, online classes are often more cost-effective than traditional classes. With traditional classes, I would have to pay for tuition, textbooks, transportation, and other expenses that can add up quickly. On the other hand, online classes usually only require payment of tuition and any necessary software or technology, which can be significantly less expensive.

Finally, online classes allow me to connect with people from all over the world. In my online classes, I have met and worked with people from different countries and cultures, which has broadened my perspective and understanding of the world. This is something that would not have been possible with traditional classes, where students are usually from the same geographic area.

Overall, I believe that online classes are the better choice for me due to their flexibility, cost-effectiveness, and global reach.

75. Should governments ban single-use plastics?

Plastic waste is becoming an increasingly pressing environmental issue. Some argue that the best way to tackle this problem is for governments to ban single-use plastics, while others believe that education and voluntary efforts are more effective.

1- Choose a side: Do you support a ban on single-use plastics, or do you believe that education and voluntary efforts are more effective?
2- Explain why you support your chosen approach.
3- Provide examples and evidence to support your argument.
4- Write about 150-200 words.

Option A: I support a ban on single-use plastics.
Option B: I believe that education and voluntary efforts are more effective.

Response:

I strongly support the idea of a ban on single-use plastics. The amount of plastic waste in our environment is overwhelming, and voluntary efforts alone are not sufficient to address this issue. The introduction of single-use plastic bans can lead to a significant reduction in the amount of plastic waste produced, and it is the responsibility of governments to take action to protect the environment.

Bans on single-use plastics have already been successful in several countries, such as France and Canada. In Canada, the federal government has announced a ban on six single-use plastic items, including straws, cutlery, and stir sticks, which will come into effect by the end of 2021. This is a significant step towards reducing plastic waste in Canada and shows that government intervention can be effective in addressing this issue.

Moreover, while education and voluntary efforts are important, they cannot be relied upon solely to reduce plastic waste. Individuals are often hesitant to change their behavior, and education and voluntary efforts can only do so much to change this. By implementing bans on single-use plastics, governments can help shift people's behavior towards more sustainable options.

In conclusion, I believe that a ban on single-use plastics is necessary to reduce plastic waste and protect the environment. Governments have a responsibility to take action, and by doing so, they can lead the way in creating a more sustainable future for us all.

76. Banning Smoking in Public Places

Smoking is a controversial topic. Some people believe that smoking should be banned in all public places while others argue that it is a personal choice and should not be regulated by law. You have been asked to write an essay discussing your position on this issue.

1- State your position: Do you believe smoking should be banned in public places, or not?
2- Explain the reasons for your position.
3- Provide specific examples and evidence to support your argument.
4- Write about 150-200 words.

Response:

I am of the opinion that smoking should be banned in all public places.

Firstly, smoking is a health hazard, not just to the smoker but also to those around them. Secondhand smoke can cause lung cancer, heart disease, and other respiratory illnesses. It is unfair to non-smokers to be exposed to this risk simply because they are in a public place. Furthermore, children and pregnant women are particularly susceptible to the dangers of secondhand smoke.

Secondly, smoking is a form of pollution. Cigarette smoke releases harmful chemicals into the air, contributing to air pollution. This pollution can have negative effects on the environment and on the health of the general public.

Finally, smoking in public places can be a fire hazard. Cigarettes can start fires if not disposed of properly, which can lead to property damage, injury, and even death.

To conclude, the risks associated with smoking in public places are too great to ignore. Banning smoking in all public places would protect the health of non-smokers, reduce pollution, and decrease the risk of fire. Smokers can still choose to smoke in their own homes or in designated smoking areas, but it should not be allowed in public places.

77. Public Transportation or Personal Vehicle?

You live in a city where there are public transportation options, such as buses and trains, but you also have a personal vehicle. Your boss has given you the option to receive a monthly stipend for public transportation or a parking spot at work. Which option would you choose?

1- Choose the option that you prefer.
2- Explain why you prefer this option.
3- Describe the benefits of your preferred option.
4- Write about 150-200 words.

Option A: Monthly stipend for public transportation.
Option B: Parking spot at work.

Response:

Thank you for providing me with the option to choose between a monthly stipend for public transportation and a parking spot at work. After careful consideration, I would like to choose the monthly stipend for public transportation.

One of the main reasons for my preference is that I believe public transportation is a more sustainable option compared to driving my own car. It reduces traffic congestion, air pollution, and greenhouse gas emissions. Moreover, it helps to save fuel and maintenance costs, which would be a financial benefit for me as well.

Another reason for choosing the public transportation option is that it can save me time and reduce stress. Driving in heavy traffic can be a frustrating experience, and finding a parking spot can be time-consuming. With public transportation, I can sit back and relax while commuting to work, and use my time more efficiently by reading or catching up on work.

Lastly, I appreciate that the monthly stipend for public transportation allows me to have more flexibility in my commute. I can choose different modes of public transportation, such as taking a bus or a train, depending on my schedule and convenience. This way, I can avoid being stuck in traffic during peak hours and arrive at work on time.

In conclusion, I believe that the monthly stipend for public transportation is the better option for me, as it not only provides financial benefits but also contributes to a more sustainable and stress-free commute. Thank you for giving me the opportunity to express my preference.

78. Should school uniforms be mandatory?

You are a high school student and the school board is considering making school uniforms mandatory for all students. Some people believe that school uniforms are a good idea, while others think that students should be able to wear their own clothes to school. The school board has asked for feedback from students, and wants you to write a response to a survey with the following prompt:

1- Do you think school uniforms should be mandatory?
2- Why or why not?
3- Give specific reasons and examples to support your answer.
4- Write about 150-200 words.

Option A: Uniforms should be mandatory
Option B: Uniforms should not be mandatory

Response:

I strongly believe that school uniforms should not be mandatory in our high school. While I
understand that school uniforms can be a great equalizer, they do not allow students to
express themselves and can actually cause more harm than good.

Firstly, students should be allowed to express themselves and wear what they feel comfortable
in. Clothing can be a form of self-expression and taking that away can have negative effects
on students' mental health. It is important that we let students be themselves and feel good
about themselves. Uniforms can be a source of embarrassment for students who may not feel
comfortable in them or cannot afford to buy new ones.

Secondly, uniforms can cause unnecessary tension and bullying amongst students. By

removing the option to wear different types of clothing, students who do not conform to the
uniform code may be singled out and bullied for being different. This is not a healthy
environment for students and can lead to a decrease in academic performance.

Finally, enforcing a uniform policy takes away from more important issues that schools need to
focus on, such as providing a quality education to students. Instead of focusing on clothing, we
should be focused on creating a welcoming and supportive environment for all students.

In conclusion, school uniforms should not be mandatory in our high school. While they may
have some benefits, they do not outweigh the negatives of removing self-expression and
creating a potentially toxic environment.

79. Buying or Renting a Home

You have saved enough money to purchase a home, but you are also considering renting a home. Write an email to your friend explaining which option you prefer and why.

1- Choose the option that you prefer (buying or renting).
2- Explain why you prefer your chosen option.
3- Describe the reasons and factors that influenced your decision.
4- Write about 150-200 words.

Option A: Buying
Option B: Renting

Response:

Dear Jane,

I hope you're doing well. As you know, I have been contemplating whether to purchase a home or to rent one. After considering all the factors, I have come to the conclusion that renting a home would be a better option for me at this point.

The main reason for this decision is the flexibility that renting offers. I'm not quite sure where my career will take me in the next few years, and I don't want to be tied down to a particular location. Additionally, I'm not quite ready for the long-term financial commitment that comes with owning a home. Renting will allow me to have more financial freedom and flexibility, while still being able to have a comfortable and stable home environment.

Other factors that influenced my decision include the maintenance and repair costs that come with owning a home. With renting, the landlord takes care of all the maintenance and repair costs, which is a huge relief. Additionally, renting allows me to have access to amenities that I wouldn't be able to afford if I were to purchase a home, such as a gym, pool, and concierge service.

Overall, I believe that renting a home is the best decision for me at this point in my life. It will allow me to have more flexibility, financial freedom, and access to amenities that I wouldn't be able to afford if I were to purchase a home. Thank you for your support and understanding.

80. City Life vs. Country Life

You are considering a move to a new place. You have the option of living in a city or living in the countryside. You are undecided and want to get opinions from people. Write a response to an opinion survey asking for your preference.

1- Choose your preference: living in a city or living in the countryside.
2- Explain why you prefer your choice.
3- Describe the benefits of living in your preferred area.
4- Write about 150-200 words.

Option A: I prefer to live in the city.
Option B: I prefer to live in the countryside.

Response:

I prefer to live in the city because of the convenience and the energy that the urban lifestyle provides. The city is where all the action is, and I thrive in a bustling environment where there is always something to do.

One of the main benefits of living in the city is the convenience it offers. Everything is within walking distance, and there is always a variety of options available. For instance, I can choose to walk to a coffee shop, a gym, a library, or a grocery store, all within a few blocks from my apartment. Public transportation is also readily available, and it is easy to get to other parts of the city or even the airport.

Another reason why I prefer city life is the energy and vibrancy that comes with it. The city is home to people from all walks of life, and it provides endless opportunities to learn, grow and experience new things. From attending concerts to trying out new foods, the city offers a diverse range of activities that can cater to all interests and hobbies.

Lastly, the city offers a wealth of career opportunities, making it an ideal place to advance one's career. As someone who is ambitious and career-driven, I find that the city provides a plethora of job opportunities, networking events, and resources that can help me grow professionally.

In conclusion, while the countryside may offer a peaceful and serene environment, I believe that the city provides a more vibrant and convenient lifestyle that aligns with my interests and goals.

81. Recycling Program

Your city is considering implementing a recycling program that requires residents to separate their waste into different categories (e.g., paper, plastics, glass, etc.) for pickup. The program would be mandatory for all households and would result in an increase in waste pickup fees. The city is conducting a survey to gather opinions from residents.

1- Choose the option that reflects your opinion on the proposed recycling program.
2- Explain the reasons for your choice.
3- Write about 150-200 words.

Option A: I support the recycling program and am willing to pay higher waste pickup fees to participate.
Option B: I do not support the recycling program and am not willing to pay higher waste pickup fees to participate.

Response:

I wholeheartedly support the proposed recycling program and I am willing to pay higher waste pickup fees to participate. There are several reasons why I believe this program would be beneficial for our city and its residents.

Firstly, implementing a recycling program would significantly reduce the amount of waste that ends up in our landfills, which is important for our environment. This would also allow us to reuse and repurpose materials, reducing the need to manufacture new products and therefore conserving natural resources.

Secondly, I believe that mandatory participation would help to create a culture of responsible waste management in our city. By requiring all residents to separate their waste into different categories, we can ensure that everyone is contributing to the collective goal of reducing our environmental impact.

Finally, I believe that the proposed increase in waste pickup fees is a small price to pay for the benefits that this program would bring. We must recognize that we all have a responsibility to protect the environment and support initiatives that promote sustainability.

In conclusion, I strongly encourage the city council to implement the recycling program and I look forward to contributing to this important effort.

82. Digital Books or Printed Books

As an avid reader, you are considering purchasing a new book. However, you can't decide whether to buy a digital book or a printed book. Some people argue that digital books are more convenient, while others claim that printed books provide a better reading experience. You decide to conduct a survey to gather opinions from others.

1- Choose whether you prefer digital or printed books.
2- Why do you prefer your choice?
3- Explain the reasons for your choice.
4- Write about 150-200 words.

Option A: I prefer digital books.
Option B: I prefer printed books.

Response:

I prefer digital books over printed books for various reasons.

Firstly, digital books are very convenient. With a digital book, I can easily carry thousands of books in one device, making it easy to take with me wherever I go. This is especially handy when traveling, as I can have a variety of books to choose from without adding extra weight to my luggage.

Secondly, digital books are environmentally friendly. By using digital books, I am not contributing to the destruction of trees and the environment. Thirdly, digital books offer various features that improve my reading experience, such as the ability to highlight, search, and bookmark sections. This makes it easier to refer back to specific sections and find information that I need.

Although printed books have their own charm, I find that digital books provide a better reading experience for me personally. I do appreciate the physical aspect of a printed book, but I find that the convenience and features of digital books outweigh this.

In addition, with digital books becoming increasingly popular, I find that many books are now only available in digital format. Overall, I believe that digital books are the way of the future and will continue to be a valuable and convenient resource for avid readers like myself.

83. Advantages and Disadvantages of Online Education

Many students today are opting for online education instead of traditional classroom education. Some people think that online education is better than classroom education, while others believe that classroom education is still the best way to learn. Write a response to the survey questions below.

1- Do you prefer online education or traditional classroom education?
2- What are the advantages and disadvantages of your preferred mode of education?
3- Explain the reasons for your choice.
4- Write about 150-200 words.

Option A: I prefer online education.
Option B: I prefer traditional classroom education.

Response:

I strongly believe that online education is a better option than traditional classroom education. The advantages of online education are numerous. First, it provides flexibility and convenience that traditional education cannot offer. Students can learn at their own pace and schedule. Second, online education offers a wider range of courses and programs, which means students have more options to choose from. Third, online education is often more affordable than traditional classroom education.

On the other hand, traditional classroom education has its own advantages. The interaction between students and teachers is more direct and personal, which can enhance the learning experience. Also, the sense of community and peer support that traditional classroom education offers is valuable and cannot be replicated in an online environment.

Despite these advantages, I still prefer online education. As a working adult, I need the flexibility to balance my work and education. Online education allows me to learn on my own schedule and at my own pace. Additionally, the affordability of online education is a huge factor for me as I cannot afford the cost of traditional classroom education. Overall, I believe that online education is the best option for people who are looking for a flexible and affordable way to pursue their education.

84- Carpooling or Driving Alone?

Your workplace is located in a congested area with limited parking spots. The management is considering implementing a carpooling program for the employees to reduce traffic congestion and parking problems. However, some employees prefer to drive alone as they value their privacy and independence. You have been asked to give your opinion on the following two options:

Option A: The carpooling program should be mandatory for all employees.
Option B: Employees should have the option to choose whether to join the carpooling program or drive alone.

Response:

I believe that option B, giving employees the option to choose whether to join the carpooling program or drive alone, is the better choice.

While a mandatory carpooling program could reduce traffic congestion and parking problems, it could also lead to resentment from employees who value their privacy and independence. This could ultimately lead to reduced employee morale and productivity.

By allowing employees to choose whether to join the carpooling program or drive alone, the company can provide a flexible and accommodating work environment that values the needs and preferences of individual employees. Some employees may prefer to carpool for social or environmental reasons, while others may prefer to drive alone for personal reasons. By giving employees the option to choose, the company can better accommodate a diverse range of employee needs and preferences.

Additionally, by promoting carpooling as an option rather than a mandatory program, the company can encourage voluntary participation and promote a positive and cooperative work environment. The company can also provide incentives, such as preferred parking spots, to employees who choose to carpool, further encouraging voluntary participation.

Overall, I believe that option B is the better choice as it provides a flexible and accommodating work environment that values the needs and preferences of individual employees while also promoting positive and cooperative behavior.

85. Company Dress Code

Your company is considering implementing a new dress code policy. Some employees have suggested that the dress code should be more relaxed to allow for more casual clothing, while others believe that the dress code should be more formal to maintain a professional atmosphere. The boss has asked you to respond to a survey to help them make the decision.

1- Choose the option that you prefer.
2- Why do you prefer your choice?
3- Explain the reasons for your choice.
4- Write about 150-200 words.

Option A: I prefer a more relaxed dress code.
Option B: I prefer a more formal dress code.

Response:

Thank you for inviting me to share my opinion on the company dress code. I believe that a more relaxed dress code would be beneficial for our company for several reasons.

Firstly, a relaxed dress code can improve employee morale and productivity. When employees are allowed to dress in a way that is comfortable and reflects their personal style, they are more likely to feel confident and motivated. This can lead to a more positive and productive work environment.

Secondly, a more relaxed dress code can make our company more attractive to job seekers. Many professionals today value work-life balance and a more casual work environment. By offering a relaxed dress code, we can position ourselves as a modern and flexible employer.

Lastly, a relaxed dress code can be cost-effective for employees. Formal business attire can be expensive, and a relaxed dress code would allow employees to wear clothes they already own. This can be especially helpful for employees who are just starting their careers and may not have the budget for expensive work clothes.

In conclusion, I believe that a more relaxed dress code would be beneficial for our company. It can improve employee morale and productivity, attract job seekers, and be cost-effective for employees. Thank you for considering my feedback.

86. Employee Benefits

Your company is considering adding a new benefit for employees. The two options being considered are a fitness allowance or a transportation allowance. The boss has asked you to respond to a survey to help them make the decision.

1- Choose the option that you prefer.
2- Why do you prefer your choice?
3- Explain the reasons for your choice.
4- Write about 150-200 words.

Option A: I believe that the company should provide a fitness allowance.
Option B: I believe that the company should provide a transportation allowance.

Response:

I am writing to express my opinion regarding the new employee benefit being considered by the company. While both options have their merits, I strongly believe that a fitness allowance would be a more valuable benefit for employees.

Firstly, a fitness allowance would help promote employee health and wellness. Encouraging employees to stay active and healthy can have many benefits for the company, including reduced healthcare costs and improved employee productivity. Studies have shown that regular exercise can help reduce stress levels and increase energy and focus, all of which can lead to better job performance.

Secondly, a fitness allowance can also improve employee satisfaction and retention. Many employees today prioritize health and wellness, and companies that offer wellness programs or fitness benefits are often more attractive to job seekers. In addition, employees who are satisfied with their benefits are more likely to stay with the company long-term.

Lastly, a fitness allowance can be a more versatile benefit compared to a transportation allowance. While transportation costs can be a significant expense for some employees, not all employees may have the same transportation needs. On the other hand, a fitness allowance can be used by all employees, regardless of their transportation situation.

In conclusion, I believe that a fitness allowance would be a valuable benefit for employees, promoting health and wellness and improving employee satisfaction and retention. Thank you for considering my feedback.

87. Office Decorations

Your company has recently moved to a new office building. The management team is asking for opinions on how to decorate the office. They have two options in mind:

Option A: Keep the office simple with minimal decorations.
Option B: Decorate the office with bright and colorful decorations.

1- Choose the option that you prefer.
2- Why do you prefer your choice?
3- Explain the reasons for your choice.
4- Write about 150-200 words.

Response:

I strongly believe that option B, which suggests decorating the office with bright and colorful decorations, would be the best choice for our new office.

Studies have shown that a well-decorated office can increase employee satisfaction, which in turn can lead to increased productivity. I have personally observed that an office with bright and colorful decorations helps to create a positive atmosphere and promotes creativity. Option B will not only make the office look more attractive, but it will also have a positive impact on the mental well-being of our employees.

Moreover, having bright and colorful decorations can help to create a welcoming environment for visitors and clients. It can also help to create a positive first impression of our company, which is important for building good relationships.

While it is true that minimal decorations may look more professional, I believe that option B can strike a balance between professionalism and creativity. We can choose decorations that are not too distracting or overwhelming, but still add some color and character to our office.

In conclusion, I strongly recommend option B for decorating our new office. I believe that it will create a positive and welcoming atmosphere, promote creativity, and improve employee satisfaction and productivity.

88. Lunch Breaks

Your company is considering changing the lunch break policy. The management team is asking for opinions on two possible options:

Option A: Keep the current lunch break policy, which allows for a one-hour break.
Option B: Shorten the lunch break to 30 minutes and allow employees to leave 30 minutes earlier at the end of the day.

1- Choose the option that you prefer.
2- Why do you prefer your choice?
3- Explain the reasons for your choice.
4- Write about 150-200 words.

Response:

I prefer option A, which suggests keeping the current lunch break policy of one hour.

Taking a lunch break is not just a time for employees to eat their meals, but also a chance to recharge and refresh their minds. A one-hour lunch break allows employees to step away from their work, relax, and come back to their tasks with renewed energy and focus. It also provides an opportunity for employees to socialize and connect with their colleagues, which can improve teamwork and morale.

On the other hand, shortening the lunch break to 30 minutes and allowing employees to leave 30 minutes earlier at the end of the day may seem like an attractive option, but it could have negative consequences. For some employees, a 30-minute break may not be sufficient to eat their meals and take a mental break. They may end up feeling rushed and stressed, which can lead to decreased productivity and job satisfaction.

Additionally, leaving 30 minutes earlier at the end of the day may not be practical for all employees, especially those who have meetings or tasks that require them to stay later. It may also cause scheduling conflicts for departments that need coverage throughout the day.

In conclusion, I strongly recommend option A for keeping the current lunch break policy of one hour. It provides employees with a much-needed break from work, promotes teamwork and morale, and can lead to increased productivity and job satisfaction.

89. Telecommuting

Your company is considering implementing a telecommuting policy. The management team is asking for opinions on two possible options:

Option A: Allow employees to work from home two days a week.
Option B: Allow employees to work from home three days a week.

1- Choose the option that you prefer.
2- Why do you prefer your choice?
3- Explain the reasons for your choice.
4- Write about 150-200 words.

Response:

I prefer option A, which allows employees to work from home two days a week.

Working from home has become increasingly popular, especially since the pandemic. It provides employees with more flexibility and can increase productivity. However, allowing employees to work from home three days a week may not be practical for all employees.

Firstly, working from home three days a week may create scheduling conflicts for some employees. Some employees may need to be present in the office on certain days to attend meetings or collaborate with colleagues. Having a set schedule of two days of telecommuting per week can provide structure and clarity for employees and management.

Secondly, working from home for three days can create isolation for some employees, which can lead to feelings of loneliness and decreased morale. Having two days in the office can provide opportunities for socialization and teamwork, which can improve morale and productivity.

Thirdly, working from home three days a week can create a blurry line between work and personal life. Employees may find it challenging to separate work from their personal lives, leading to burnout and decreased job satisfaction.

In conclusion, I recommend option A, allowing employees to work from home two days a week. It provides flexibility while maintaining structure and collaboration in the office. It can also improve morale and productivity while avoiding burnout and isolation.

90. In person Meetings or Online Meetings

Your company is considering a new policy that would require all meetings to be conducted online. Some employees are in favor of this change, while others prefer in-person meetings. Your boss has asked you to respond to an opinion survey.

Choose the option that you prefer.
Why do you prefer your choice?
Explain the reasons for your choice.
Write about 150-200 words.

Option A: I think we should stick to in-person meetings.
Option B: I think we should conduct all meetings online.

Response:

I strongly believe that in-person meetings are more effective than online meetings and we should stick to this format. There are several reasons why I think this is the best option for our company.

Firstly, in-person meetings provide greater opportunities for effective communication and collaboration. Nonverbal cues, such as facial expressions and body language, play an important role in communication and are more difficult to interpret in an online setting. This can lead to misunderstandings and less effective collaboration. In-person meetings also provide opportunities for spontaneous discussions and brainstorming, which can lead to more creative solutions.

Secondly, in-person meetings can help to build stronger relationships between employees. Face-to-face interactions can help to establish trust and rapport, which are important for effective teamwork and collaboration. Online meetings can be impersonal and may not provide the same opportunities for socializing and team-building.

On the other hand, I understand that online meetings can be

more convenient and cost-effective, especially for employees who work remotely or in different locations. However, I believe that the benefits of in-person meetings outweigh the convenience and cost savings of online meetings.

In conclusion, I strongly believe that we should stick to in-person meetings for our company. They provide greater opportunities for effective communication and collaboration, help to build stronger relationships between employees, and promote creativity and innovation.

91. Email or Phone Calls

Your boss is considering a new policy that would require all communication with clients to be conducted through email instead of phone calls. Some employees are in favor of this change, while others prefer communicating with clients over the phone. Your boss has asked you to respond to an opinion survey.

1- Choose the option that you prefer.
2- Why do you prefer your choice?
3- Explain the reasons for your choice.
4- Write about 150-200 words.

Option A: I think we should continue communicating with clients over the phone.
Option B: I think we should communicate with clients through email instead of phone calls.

Response:

I strongly believe that we should continue communicating with clients over the phone instead of switching to email. While I understand that email communication can be convenient and efficient, I believe that phone calls provide several benefits that are crucial for our business.

Firstly, phone calls allow for more effective communication and problem-solving. Unlike email, phone calls provide the opportunity for immediate feedback and clarification. This can help to resolve issues more quickly and efficiently, leading to better outcomes for our clients and our business.

Secondly, phone calls can help to build stronger relationships with our clients. Personal connections are important in business, and phone calls allow for a more personal and human connection. This can help to build trust and rapport with our clients, which can lead to better client retention and increased business opportunities.

Finally, phone calls can help to prevent misunderstandings and miscommunications. Tone of voice and inflection are important elements of communication that are lost in written communication. This can lead to misunderstandings or hurt feelings, which can be detrimental to our business relationships.

In conclusion, while email communication may be convenient and efficient, I strongly believe that we should continue communicating with our clients over the phone. Phone calls provide more effective communication and problem-solving, help to build stronger relationships, and can prevent misunderstandings and miscommunications.

92. Workplace Diversity

Your company is considering implementing a diversity training program for all employees. Some employees are in favor of the program, while others believe it is unnecessary. Your employer has asked you to respond to an opinion survey.

1- Choose the option that you prefer.
2- Why do you prefer your choice?
3- Explain the reasons for your choice.
4- Write about 150-200 words.

Option A: I think the diversity training program is unnecessary.
Option B: I think the diversity training program is important and necessary.

Response:

I am in favor of implementing a diversity training program for all employees. While I understand that some employees may believe that such a program is unnecessary, I believe that it is important for several reasons.

Firstly, a diversity training program can help to promote a more inclusive workplace culture. By educating employees on topics such as unconscious bias, cultural competence, and diversity and inclusion best practices, we can create a more welcoming environment for all employees, regardless of their background or identity.

Secondly, a diversity training program can help to prevent discrimination and harassment in the workplace. By ensuring that all employees are aware of their rights and responsibilities with regards to workplace conduct, we can create a safer and more respectful workplace for all.

Finally, a diversity training program can have business benefits. Studies have shown that diverse and inclusive workplaces are more innovative and productive, leading to better financial outcomes for the company.

In conclusion, while some employees may believe that a diversity training program is unnecessary, I believe that it is important and necessary for promoting a more inclusive workplace culture, preventing discrimination and harassment, and improving business outcomes. I would be happy to participate in such a program and believe that it could be a valuable investment for our company.

93. Social Media Use in the Workplace

Your employer has noticed that some employees spend a significant amount of time on social media during work hours. Some employees argue that social media use can be a valuable tool for networking and promoting the company, while others believe that it is a distraction and can negatively impact productivity. Your employer has asked you to respond to an opinion survey.

1- Choose the option that you prefer.
2- Why do you prefer your choice?
3- Explain the reasons for your choice.
4- Write about 150-200 words.

Option A: I think social media use during work hours should be prohibited.
Option B: I think social media use during work hours should be allowed.

Response:

I believe that social media use during work hours should be allowed, but with certain limitations. While it is true that social media can be a distraction and can negatively impact productivity, it can also be a valuable tool for networking and promoting the company.

Firstly, social media can be used to build and maintain professional networks, which can be beneficial for both the employee and the company. By connecting with industry professionals and potential customers, employees can expand their knowledge and reach, and can also help to promote the company's brand and products.

Secondly, social media can be used as a marketing and advertising tool. With the right strategies and content, social media can be an effective way to reach new customers and engage with existing ones. This can help to increase brand awareness and sales, which ultimately benefits the company.

However, I believe that social media use should be restricted to certain times and for certain purposes. For example, employees could be allowed to use social media during breaks or outside of regular work hours, and social media use should be limited to professional networking and marketing purposes only. Additionally, employees should be made aware of the company's social media policies and expectations, and should be held accountable for any inappropriate or unproductive social media use during work hours.

In conclusion, while social media use can be a distraction and can negatively impact productivity, it can also be a valuable tool for networking and promoting the company. By setting clear guidelines and expectations, and allowing social media use for professional purposes only, the company can benefit from the advantages of social media without sacrificing productivity.

94. Overtime Pay or Extra Time Off?

Your company is considering offering either overtime pay or extra time off as compensation for working beyond regular hours. Some employees prefer to receive overtime pay, while others prefer to receive extra time off. The company has asked you to respond to an opinion survey.

1- Choose the option that you prefer.
2- Why do you prefer your choice?
3- Explain the reasons for your choice.
4- Write about 150-200 words.

Option A: I prefer to receive overtime pay.
Option B: I prefer to receive extra time off.

Response:

I prefer to receive extra time off instead of overtime pay as compensation for working beyond regular hours.

I believe that extra time off provides a better work-life balance and allows employees to recharge their batteries. It also gives them the opportunity to spend quality time with their families and friends, engage in leisure activities, and pursue personal interests that they may not have time for during regular work weeks.

Moreover, extra time off is often more valuable than overtime pay, as it allows employees to plan vacations or long weekends without compromising their work. In contrast, overtime pay is often taxed at a higher rate and may not be as valuable as extra time off.

Another benefit of extra time off is that it promotes employee well-being and reduces stress levels. It also encourages employees to maintain a healthy work-life balance, which in turn boosts productivity and job satisfaction.

Overall, I believe that offering extra time off as compensation for working beyond regular hours is a more effective way to retain employees and promote their well-being, which benefits both the employees and the company.

95. Flexible Work Schedule or Fixed Work Schedule?

Your company is considering offering employees the option of having a flexible work schedule or a fixed work schedule. Some employees prefer a fixed work schedule, while others prefer a flexible work schedule. The company has asked you to respond to an opinion survey.

1- Choose the option that you prefer.
2- Why do you prefer your choice?
3- Explain the reasons for your choice.
4- Write about 150-200 words.

Option A: I prefer a fixed work schedule.
Option B: I prefer a flexible work schedule.

Response:

I prefer a flexible work schedule over a fixed work schedule.

A flexible work schedule allows me to better balance my personal and professional life, and it increases my productivity and motivation. I am able to adapt my schedule to my personal needs and priorities, which allows me to achieve a better work-life balance. For example, I can work earlier or later in the day to attend to personal matters, such as appointments or family obligations.

Moreover, a flexible work schedule allows me to work when I am most productive and efficient, which increases my output and helps me accomplish tasks more effectively. I can also take breaks during the day to engage in physical activities or other leisure activities that help me recharge and stay focused.

Additionally, a flexible work schedule allows me to avoid rush hour traffic, which reduces my stress levels and saves me valuable time. It also allows me to work remotely, which eliminates the need for a physical workspace and saves the company money on rent and utility bills.

In summary, I believe that a flexible work schedule offers many benefits to both the employee and the company, and I strongly support its implementation.

96. Monthly Salary or Hourly Wage?

Your company is considering offering employees the option of being paid a monthly salary or an hourly wage. Some employees prefer a monthly salary, while others prefer an hourly wage. The company has asked you to respond to an opinion survey.

1- Choose the option that you prefer.
2- Why do you prefer your choice?
3- Explain the reasons for your choice.
4- Write about 150-200 words.

Option A: I prefer to be paid a monthly salary.
Option B: I prefer to be paid an hourly wage.

Response:

I prefer to be paid a monthly salary over being paid an hourly wage.

Being paid a monthly salary provides me with financial stability and predictability. I can better plan and budget my expenses without worrying about fluctuations in my income due to differences in the number of hours worked. A monthly salary also provides me with a steady income stream that allows me to make long-term financial commitments, such as buying a home or saving for retirement.

Moreover, being paid a monthly salary allows me to focus on my job responsibilities and performance, rather than worrying about the number of hours I work. I can better balance my work and personal life without having to worry about losing income due to taking time off for personal reasons, such as illness or family obligations.

Additionally, being paid a monthly salary promotes a more collaborative and team-oriented work environment. It encourages employees to work together to achieve common goals, rather than competing with each other for hours or overtime pay.

In summary, I believe that being paid a monthly salary offers many benefits to both the employee and the company, and I fully support its implementation as an alternative to being paid an hourly wage.

97. Physical or Online Shopping?

Your local store is considering expanding its online shopping options, while still keeping its physical store open. Some customers prefer shopping in-store, while others prefer shopping online. The store has asked you to respond to an opinion survey.

1- Choose the option that you prefer.
2- Why do you prefer your choice?
3- Explain the reasons for your choice.
4- Write about 150-200 words.

Option A: I prefer shopping in-store.
Option B: I prefer shopping online.

Response:

I prefer shopping online instead of shopping in-store.

Shopping online offers greater convenience, as it allows me to shop from the comfort of my home, at any time of the day or night. It also eliminates the need to travel to the store, find a parking spot, and wait in line at the checkout. Additionally, online shopping offers a wider variety of products, as I can easily browse through different websites to find the exact item I am looking for.

Moreover, online shopping provides a safer option during the pandemic, as it minimizes the risk of exposure to the virus by reducing contact with people in crowded spaces.

Another benefit of online shopping is the ability to compare prices and read reviews from other customers, which helps me make an informed decision before making a purchase. This is particularly useful for big-ticket items, where I want to ensure that I am getting the best value for my money.

However, I do understand the importance of having a physical store for certain aspects of shopping, such as the ability to touch and feel products before making a purchase. Therefore, I believe that a hybrid model, where customers can choose to shop online or come into the store as needed, would be the most ideal solution.

In conclusion, I believe that online shopping offers many benefits to customers, and I support its expansion as an additional shopping option.

98. Electronic Books or Printed Books?

With the rise of technology, electronic books have become increasingly popular and accessible. However, there are still many readers who prefer the traditional printed books. Your local library is considering expanding their e-book collection and has asked you to respond to an opinion survey.

1- Choose the option that you prefer.
2- Why do you prefer your choice?
3- Explain the reasons for your choice.
4- Write about 150-200 words.

Option A: I prefer electronic books.
Option B: I prefer printed books.

Response:

I prefer electronic books over printed books.

Electronic books offer many advantages over traditional printed books. Firstly, they are portable and convenient, as I can carry an entire library of books on my tablet or e-reader without adding any extra weight to my bag. This is particularly useful when traveling or commuting, as it eliminates the need to carry heavy books around.

Secondly, e-books are often cheaper than printed books, as they eliminate the costs associated with printing and distribution. This allows me to read more books without breaking my budget.

Thirdly, e-books offer a customizable reading experience, as I can adjust the font size, background color, and lighting to suit my preferences. This is particularly beneficial for readers with visual impairments, who may struggle to read traditional printed books.

Lastly, e-books are more environmentally friendly, as they eliminate the need for paper and ink, and reduce the carbon footprint associated with shipping and transportation.

However, I do understand the importance of printed books, particularly for collectors and those who prefer the tactile experience of reading. Therefore, I believe that a hybrid model, where the library offers both printed and electronic books, would be the most ideal solution.

In conclusion, I believe that electronic books offer many benefits to readers, and I support their expansion as an additional reading option in the library.

99. Summer or Winter Vacation?

Your school is considering changing the current academic calendar to offer students a longer break during either the summer or winter. They have asked you to respond to an opinion survey.

1- Choose the option that you prefer.
2- Why do you prefer your choice?
3- Explain the reasons for your choice.
4- Write about 150-200 words.

Option A: I prefer a longer summer break.
Option B: I prefer a longer winter break.

Response:

I believe that a longer summer break would be more beneficial for students.

Summer vacation provides a unique opportunity for students to engage in activities that promote learning outside of the classroom. Students have more time to explore their interests, pursue internships, volunteer, and gain practical experience that can help them in their future careers. Additionally, the longer summer break would allow students to spend more quality time with their families, travel, and experience new cultures, which can broaden their horizons and deepen their understanding of the world.

On the other hand, a longer winter break can have some drawbacks. It often falls during the holiday season when many families are already taking time off work, and there may be limited opportunities for students to engage in activities that promote learning. Also, the winter break may be more challenging for students who have to travel long distances or endure harsh weather conditions to reach their destinations.

In conclusion, I believe that a longer summer break would be the better option for students. It provides ample opportunities for students to engage in activities that promote learning and personal growth, and allows them to enjoy some much-needed relaxation and time with their families.

100. Learning a New Language or a New Skill?

Your company is offering to pay for employees to take either a language course or a skill course of their choice. They have asked you to respond to an opinion survey.

1- Choose the option that you prefer.
2- Why do you prefer your choice?
3- Explain the reasons for your choice.
4- Write about 150-200 words.

Option A: I prefer to take a language course.
Option B: I prefer to take a skill course.

Response:

Thank you for giving me the opportunity to express my opinion on whether I would prefer to take a language course or a skill course. I have given this matter some thought, and I would choose to take a language course.

Firstly, learning a new language has many benefits. It can improve communication skills, enhance cultural understanding, and provide more opportunities for personal and professional growth. As our company has clients from all over the world, it would be beneficial to have employees who can communicate effectively in different languages, which would ultimately improve the company's overall success.

Secondly, taking a language course would also be a fun and interesting experience. I have always been fascinated by different cultures and languages, and taking a course would give me the chance to explore that interest while also gaining new skills. It would be a valuable and rewarding experience that could have a positive impact on my personal and professional life.

While I understand that taking a skill course would also be beneficial, I believe that learning a new language would have a greater impact on both my personal and professional development. Therefore, I would choose to take a language course if given the opportunity.

Manufactured by Amazon.ca
Acheson, AB